NORTHERN IRELAND:
A PSYCHOLOGICAL ANALYSIS

KEN HESKIN

NORTHERN IRELAND: A PSYCHOLOGICAL ANALYSIS

Columbia University Press
New York   1980

Library of Congress Cataloging in Publication Data

Heskin, Ken.
  Northern Ireland, a psychological analysis.

  Bibliography: p.158
  Includes index.
  1. Northern Ireland—Social conditions. 2. Terrorism—
Northern Ireland—Psychological aspects. 3. Terrorism—
Psychological aspects—case studies.
Ir. Title.
HN398.I7H47   941.6   80-13407
ISBN 0-231-05138-7

To my wife, Sue,
who married into the Irish problem

Contents

Acknowledgements

Writing a book, I have discovered, is a little like having a baby. The idea and the initial commitment are exciting but then you have a long time to ponder the wisdom of your actions. During that time, many people have helped me in various ways, directly and indirectly, in arriving at this point.

I would like to thank An Bord Scoláireachtaí Cómalairte (The Scholarship Exchange Board) for their confidence in awarding me a Fulbright Fellowship to the United States, during the tenure of which I began seriously to research this book and completed first drafts of early chapters. I would also like to pay tribute to the Board's concern and efficiency in administering the fellowship on my behalf.

I am grateful to my employers, Trinity College, Dublin, for allowing me leave of absence during the tenure of my fellowship. I must thank in particular Mr Gerry Giltrap, Secretary to the College, for his kindness and consideration in dealing with the several administrative and other problems to which this absence gave rise.

Equally, I am grateful to the University of California at Davis, and the Department of Psychology in particular, for hosting my stay in the United States and enabling me to be both productive and relaxed in my new working environment.

I would particularly like to thank Alan Elms of the Department of Psychology at U.C. Davis for his guidance and advice, but above all for his encouragement and support at various critical stages of this book. I owe him much. Similarly, I would like to thank Jerry Harbison of the Economic and Social Statistics Unit, Department of Finance, Stormont for his encouragement and constructive criticism and also Ed Cairns of the

A*

Department of Psychology, New University of Ulster for his helpful comments and constant support.

I would also like to thank Mike Moore, with whom I shared an office in U.C. Davis and off whose head I frequently bounced my first thoughts on topics engaging my attention at the time; I invariably found them much improved on the rebound. I must also express my gratitude to Gill and Macmillan and to their anonymous reader, not only for encouragement at the planning stages of this book, but also for help and shrewd advice throughout. At the end of the day, however, the responsibility for the views and interpretations put forward here are mine alone.

Eilleen McGlade of Trinity College Library made efforts above and beyond the call of duty to facilitate my research and I thank her sincerely.

Finally, I must thank my wife, Sue, for her forbearance during these past two years. She has shared with me the ups and downs involved in writing this book from initial idea to finished typescript. She has carefully typed all of the various drafts involved and has saved me from many lapses of sense and grammar. She has borne these burdens while maintaining her characteristic good humour and domestic efficiency and I am profoundly grateful to her.

Ken Heskin
Trinity College
Dublin
May 1979

Introduction

As a child in peaceful Northern Ireland, I recall being frequently puzzled by some of the things people said about other people of a different religion. As I grew older, puzzlement lapsed into acceptance and acceptance eventually transformed into questioning, rejection, anger and sadness that fine, kind and decent people, my people, should harbour in their hearts feelings and attitudes unworthy of their generous spirit. Above all, I think that it is this essentially contradictory element in Northern Irish affairs which has fascinated and involved me, for as long as I can remember.

For me, the problem in Northern Ireland has always been psychological, long before I knew what the word meant. While history, politics and so forth helped to explain why people felt and behaved as they did, in the final analysis it was those feelings and behaviours, the psychology of the problem, with which I had to deal at a personal and practical level. I retain the view that, in practical terms, this is the appropriate level at which attention should be focused.

In this analysis, I have tried to apply the science of psychology, particularly social psychology, to the elucidation and understanding of why people feel and behave as they do in Northern Ireland. I have tried to use a psychological approach in the broadest possible sense and have not felt constrained in the use of psychological insights arising outside the strict academic confines of experimental psychology. There is a tendency in some academic circles to regard life as an irritating and unnecessary complication of the behaviour of subjects in psychological experiments. I have left that philosophy at peace in its particular cul-de-sac and drawn on the views of historians, economists, geographers, psychiatrists, sociologists, journalists and others as well as experimental psychologists in constructing a psychological picture of the Northern Irish situation.

I regard the topic of Northern Ireland as much too important to warrant the waste of time and energy in writing a book which would be intelligible only to other psychologists. This book is intended for the non-psychologist or layman as well as for the student of psychology. I have tried to minimise the technicalities of language and explanation for the former without over-simplifying the analysis for the latter. For any failures in either objective, I apologise.

Inevitably in writing on issues of deep feeling and concern to so many people, it is impossible (and probably unwise) to avoid comments and conclusions which some may find disagreeable or even offensive. It is not my purpose or intention to be either but merely to contribute to an understanding of the situation in Northern Ireland and to identify, realistically and objectively, important psychological influences and tensions within that situation.

Finally, I have used the terms 'Northern Ireland', 'Ulster', 'the Six Counties', 'the North of Ireland' and 'the North' interchangeably to relieve stylistic monotony. For the same simple reason, I have variously referred to the rest of Ireland as 'the Republic of Ireland', 'the South of Ireland', 'the Republic' and 'the South'.

CHAPTER ONE

Ulster Perspectives

'I want to see a public man come forward and say what the Irish question is.'

Benjamin Disraeli.

Disraeli's point, that one must define the Irish problem before one can attempt a solution to it, is as valid today as it was a century ago. The issue, however, becomes more complex when those defining the problem are interested national groups and their 'public men'. In such circumstances definitions of the problem may themselves become part of the problem in so far as they produce inconsistent or inappropriate responses to it.

Rose (1976) has come to the paralysing conclusion that 'The problem is that there is no solution.' The thrust of this chapter will rather be that no single solution is capable of accommodating the diversity of problems as defined by the main interested national groups.

A thoughtful critical appraisal of current political and academic analyses of the Northern Irish problem has been put forward by Whyte (1978). The purpose here will be to undertake the rather more nebulous, but none the less important, task of determining the characteristic outlooks of people in the Republic of Ireland, Great Britain and the United States of America to the problem.

To this end, a picture must be pieced together in each case from the results of relevant public opinion or attitude surveys, political pronouncements, media reaction, a knowledge of recent historical interactions and the combination of personal experience and intuition. Each of these is a fickle ally in any task and the result is an impression, no more or less than that. With that in mind, we now turn to the Northern Irish problem as seen in the Republic of Ireland, Great Britain and the United States.

The Irish-British Problem

While the locus of the Northern Irish problem is beyond doubt for most of its observers, the Irish have tended to see the problem not as residing in Northern Ireland, much less the Irish Republic, but rather in Great Britain. This fact alone gives a unique colouring to the Irish view of the Northern Irish problem, for it becomes for them the British problem.

The first difficulty with the Irish view of the British is in trying to decide exactly who the British are. The whole question of who constitutes a psychological 'Brit' for the Irish, North or South, is riddled with contradiction, complexity and confusion. Let us, therefore, tread lightly through the labyrinth of the Irish British problem.

Who, then are the British? To be fair, the British government itself is not quite sure and the Home Office is seeking ideas on the matter (Cmd. 6795, presented to Parliament in April 1977). Addressing this problem recently, Miller (1978) illustrates the difficulties:

> 'One thing that the Home Office, however, is certain about is that there are no such creatures as "British Citizens". There are United Kingdom citizens, who are also citizens of the colonies; but, apparently, neither the United Kingdom nor the colonies can be equated with "British", although citizens of the United Kingdom and colonies, when they sally forth on their foreign travels, are bearers of "British" not "United Kingdom" passports.' (p.16)

The United Kingdom comprises England, Scotland, Wales and Northern Ireland. Prior to 1922, the United Kingdom comprised England, Scotland, Wales and all of Ireland. Because of its multinational nature, combining as it does four countries, there has always tended to be a centrifugal aspect of Britishness, even during times of great British cohesiveness. This is illustrated in the words of a song popular among World War I British troops, *It's a long way to Tipperary*, still cherished and sung, now somewhat inappropriately, in sentimental reminiscence in England today.

At a more practical level, the wavering fortunes of Scottish and Welsh nationalist movements indicate the ambivalence of Britishness to inhabitants of those parts of Great Britain. Even within England, the resentment generated by the historical concentration of power, money and influence in the South East of England is indicative of this theme.

If the inhabitants of Great Britain (England, Scotland and Wales) are somewhat equivocal in their Britishness, it is perhaps not surprising that that confusion and contradiction is reflected in Irish attitudes to the British. A further immediate complication arises from the fact that the Irish are the third largest ethnic group in Great Britain after the English and the Scots. There are more Irish people living, working and voting in Great Britain than there are Welsh people (*World Almanac*, 1978).

The Irish in Britain, most particularly through the Labour Party and trades union movement, form an electoral power bloc out of proportion to their numbers, capable of deciding thirty or so (approximately 5 per cent) of the seats at Westminster (O'Connor, 1974) while they account for less than half of that in terms of population. The advent of a Labour government in the United Kingdom in 1964 gave a major impetus to immigrant Irish involvement in and commitment to British politics, especially since so many significant figures in the Labour Party have Irish connections. Indeed, the Prime Minister and the Chancellor of the Exchequer of the last Labour government, James Callaghan and Denis Healey, are both of Irish descent, as their names suggest.

The point of this digression into the topic of the Irish in Britain is to illustrate the difficulty which has latterly arisen for the Irish in Ireland in regard to maintaining anti-British feeling. It has not been easy to maintain the old Republican 'Brits out' mentality when the 'Brits' were led by an amiable man called Callaghan, no less, who was elected partly as a result of the votes of Irishmen in Britain, overwhelmingly cast in favo r of the Labour Party in recent years (Markham, 1971). However, some press reports have claimed that the lack of initiative of Mr Callaghan's government in Northern Ireland, perhaps highlighted by the criticisms of the Speaker of the United States House of Representatives, Mr 'Tip' O'Neill just before the election, drastically reduced Irish support for the Labour Party in the election of 3 May 1979. At the time of writing, it remains to be seen what initiatives or changes in policy will be undertaken by the Conservative government at Westminster and what the reaction of the Irish, both in Britain and Ireland, will be to them.

Historically, the tide of changing fortunes and the progression of events have removed many of the underpinnings of anti-British feeling in Ireland. While Britain has always been central to Irish history, Ireland has impinged on Britain only occasionally and is merely one aspect, in truth rather tedious, mundane and domestic, of the exciting panorama which once was the British Empire. With the decline of that empire, the economic deterioration of Britain on the one hand and the economic improvement of Ireland on the other, the turning of both countries to the new horizons of the European Economic Community and the close economic and cultural links which the countries share, the notion of Britain as neighbour and partner has been difficult to resist.

The old Republican theory that England's misfortune is Ireland's opportunity has found few takers in practice. The theory, untested for half a century, that the Irish question could be resolved if only the British would up and leave and allow the Dublin government to take over what was rightfully theirs, died, albeit after a protracted illness, among the embers and coffins of Ulster in recent years. Myths do die in Ireland, but the Irish have a peculiar respect for the dead.

It is in this particularly Irish sense that one must try to understand the Irish approach to the British and hence to the Northern Irish problem. Because, to the observer, the Irish can often appear inconsistent or hypocritical when, in fact, they are merely pursuing their own idiosyncratic ethos to its utterly logical conclusion. In particular, to Irish leaders falls the responsibility of ensuring that the appearances of dead myths are maintained while the Irish themselves get on with the business of coping with reality. Cruise O'Brien (1972) has given examples of this attitude in regard to domestic affairs and has since fallen foul of it himself as a result of his disrespect as a T.D. (member of parliament in Ireland) for Irish myths, both living and dead.

In terms of relations between Britain and Ireland, the best example of apparent inconsistency was the decision of the Irish government under de Valera in the Second World War to remain neutral, an indefensible and incomprehensible decision seen from the British perspective. From the Irish perspective, however, it was an act of political genius. On the one hand, it not only maintained the myth that the infant Republic of Ireland was a fully independent and sovereign state, it actually flaunted it in the face of the old oppressor, the British government. On the other hand, it so enabled the Irish individually and voluntarily to assist their neighbours in Great Britain, which they did in their thousands, that they merited special mention in Churchill's victory speech. (A U.K. permit office was also opened in Dublin, with the co-operation of the Dublin government, through which Irish labour could strategically be employed in the domestic war effort in Great Britain.)

The Irish attitude to Northern Ireland, therefore, has to be seen in this context. The focus of political objections to the British in Ulster turned gradually, as events in Ulster unfolded, from the fact of British 'occupation' to the form of British occupation, the torture of suspects during interrogation, the harassment of civilians, the conditions of internment camps and so forth. The myth of the validity of a simple take-over from Dublin passed quietly away in a long winter of Northern discontent and the task of the politicians in Dublin was to accommodate that fact to a sense of appropriate respect for its memory. Thus could Bowyer Bell write in 1976 'The prospect of a united Ireland with one million angry and violent Protestants and half that number of violent and radicalised Catholics holds little charm for the comfortable in Dublin. No one wants a united Ireland but the IRA.' (p. 511)

So far, this discussion has been at the level of generalities, of things which seem (to me) generally true but are obviously not absolutely true in the sense that they, even notionally, apply to everyone in the Republic of Ireland. There are, of course, people whose views would not correspond with those outlined above but who would adopt a radically different attitude to the British and to Northern Ireland. Fortunately, however, some recent research has been carried out which gives both credence and some quantitative accuracy to the above impressions.

McGreil (1977) undertook a major study of intergroup attitudes on a representative sample of almost three thousand Greater Dublin residents in 1972–73. He used the Bogardus Social Distance Scale (Bogardus, 1925, 1933) to measure affinities and aversions to a wide range of specified social groups, supplemented by a number of more conventional attitude scales or questionnaires.

The Bogardus Social Distance Scale requires the respondent

to indicate on a seven-point scale the degree of social contact which he or she would be prepared to accept with a typical member of a specified social group. The categories of social distance which were presented ran from 'Would welcome as a member of my family' through five stages of decreasing social acceptance to 'Would debar or deport from Ireland'.

McGreil found, using these measures, that his sample had a very positive attitude towards the British in general, particularly the English. Indeed 87·3 per cent of the sample indicated that they would admit English people to their family and the results indicated a preference for the English above the Northern Irish, the Welsh and the Scottish, all of whom were more socially acceptable than other European nationalities such as the French, Spanish and Italians. It is interesting to note that the high regard in which the Irish hold the English transcends ties which might have been presumed to exist on the basis of : religious similarity (the French, Spanish and Italians were all rated lower); ethnic similarity (the Celtic Scots, Welsh and Northern Irish were rated lower); historical political opposition (as O'Farrell, 1975, notes, the strongest opposition to Home Rule for Ireland came from England, whereas Scotland and Wales tended to produce a majority of Home Rulers); and finally, current politico-territorial disputes (the English are rated above the Northern Irish).

This positive view of the British was reinforced by responses to more specific questions put forward during the interviews. For example 89 per cent of McGreil's subjects agreed with the statement that 'The British are pretty decent people' and 83 per cent disagreed with the statement that 'I would never marry a British person'. These results are very clear cut and support the broad sweep of the generalisations made earlier. However, nuances and divergencies of opinion emerged in responses to other questions.

Thirty-six per cent agreed with the proposition that 'I don't object to the British people but I don't like the British government'. Fifty-five per cent disagreed with this statement but, because of the wording, this disagreement is difficult to interpret. Does it mean that all 55 per cent do not object to the British people but like the government, or that all 55 per cent do object to the British people but like the government, or that all 55 per cent do like the people and the government, or are there inestimable proportions of the 55 per cent distributed over all these possibilities? There is no way of telling but what is clear, is that at least a third of the sample saw a distinction between the British people and the British government. Similarly, about two-thirds (62 per cent) of the sample disagreed with the statement that 'The world owes a lot to Britain.'

These response patterns indicate that while there is a general and widespread positive attitude towards the British there is no generally held and pervasive identification with them. And McGreil's results do suggest a hard-core of opinion against Britain of the order of ten to 20 per cent. For example, 14·2 per cent agreed that 'British people are slow and unimaginative', 14·4 per cent agreed that they 'would never marry a British person' and 17·1 per cent indicated that they 'would be happy if Britain were brought to her knees'. (14 per cent disagreed with the proposition that 'I have no particular love or hate for the British', but, again, because of the wording, this result is un-interpretable).

The statement of perhaps most direct relevance to the British presence in Northern Ireland was that 'British soldiers are gener-ally cruel and brutal'. Interestingly, while no other statement about the British produced a percentage of 'don't know' responses in double figures, 15·1 per cent of respondents put themselves in this category for this question. Twenty-eight per cent agreed with the proposition while 57 per cent disagreed. Again this illustrates the tendency to distinguish between British institutions and British people. More particularly, since 72 per cent of respondents did not take the traditionally 'easy' course of agreeing with the proposition, it indicates a generally hard-headed approach to the problem of Northern Ireland and a re-luctance to relapse into traditional, simplistic versions of the truth.

This outlook is illustrated very clearly in responses to state-ments concerning Northern Ireland and the Northern Irish. Fifty-nine per cent agreed that 'Catholics in Northern Ireland have more in common with Northern Protestants than they have with Catholics in the Republic'. Similarly, 53 per cent disagreed that 'Northern Irish Protestants have more in common with the rest of Irish people than they have with the British'. Eighty-five per cent agreed that 'Protestants in the Republic have more in common with Catholics here than they have with Protestants in Northern Ireland.' Fifty-five per cent agreed that

'Northerners on all sides tend to be extreme and unreasonable.'

All of these response patterns indicate a majority rejection of simple, old-fashioned Gaelic nationalism in practice. And yet, 64 per cent regarded the old nationalist political solution of a thirty-two county Republic with one central government as desirable, the clearly most preferred political solution. In addition, 55 per cent disagreed with the proposition that 'Northern Ireland and the Republic are two separate nations'. Thus are dead myths respected.

The question of how representative McGreil's subjects were of Ireland as a whole is important. The fact is that they were residents of the Greater Dublin area and hence, one might suppose that they would represent rather more sophisticated views than would be general in rural Ireland or in less cosmopolitan Irish conurbations. However the rate of growth of population in Dublin in recent years, largely represented by movement from the provinces, has been quite startling. On this basis, Cruise O'Brien (1978) has argued that McGreil's results may be reasonably representative of Ireland as a whole. Given that over a quarter of the population of the Republic of Ireland lives in the Dublin area, and taking Cruise O'Brien's point into account, it is clear that McGreil's results are an important indicator of Irish attitudes generally.

Rose, McAllister and Mair (1978) have concluded, on the basis of a comprehensive review of public opinion surveys in Northern Ireland, the Republic and Great Britain, that Irish unity 'is not a "pie in the sky" idea, remote from this world' (p. 36–37). But such public opinion surveys frequently ask 'surface' questions which members of the public can answer spontaneously, if not unthinkingly. Those surveys which have presented the issue of Irish unity to the southern Irish public alongside some of its likely attendant problems have found the usual unequivocal endorsement level of 60 per cent—70 per cent drop to less than half that level when the public is obliged to consider the consequences of that eventuality (Rose, McAllister and Mair, 1978, p. 35–37). Furthermore, McGreil's data, probing the issues considerably further than the typical public opinion survey, support the contention put forward here that Irish unity *is*, in many important respects, a 'pie in the sky' idea for the people of the Irish Republic.

A very recent and controversial survey published by the Economic and Social Research Institute (ESRI) in Dublin (Davis and Sinnott, 1979) set out to examine attitudes in the Republic to the Northern Ireland problem. This nationwide survey conducted between July and September 1978 found a predictable 68 per cent in favour of Irish unity, either in the form of a one-government state (41 per cent) or a federal arrangement (27 per cent). Moreover 78 per cent agreed with the proposition that the British government should announce its intention to withdraw from Northern Ireland at a fixed date in the future, and 71 per cent thought that the British government should declare its intention to withdraw 'whether the majority in Northern Ireland agrees or not'.

The problem with taking these findings as an indication of what people in the Republic would really like to happen, as opposed to what they say they would like to happen, is that these questions were posed before respondents were invited to consider the difficulties of such eventualities actually occurring. As Rose, McAllister and Mair's data indicate, this arrangement of questions considerably distorts the picture.

When we look at the responses reported in the survey to statements which raise the question of the attendant difficulties of British withdrawal and Irish unity, then we can see that a more hard-headed, less simplistic picture of the problem lies just below the surface of public opinion in the Republic. For example, it seems quite literally true that the Irish in the South are somewhat chary of putting their money where their mouth is; 51 per cent indicated that they would not be prepared to pay heavier taxes to run a united Ireland.

Sixty per cent agreed that in the event of a united Ireland, 'Loyalist paramilitaries would be more of a problem than the IRA is today'. Equally, 59 per cent thought that 'British withdrawal from Northern Ireland without the consent of the parties involved would lead to a great increase in violence'. Forty-three per cent felt that withdrawal without consent would lead to a negotiated settlement. Analysing the responses to both of these statements, which at first glance appear to be contradictory, Davis and Sinnott found that the contradiction was cleared up by the fact that 21 per cent felt that British withdrawal would lead to a great increase in violence and a negotiated settlement, presumably when the dust had settled. Twenty-two per cent felt that only a negotiated settlement would ensue, 11 per cent felt that neither violence nor settlement would ensue and 10 per cent 'didn't know'. However, there remained a sizable proportion (37 per cent) who felt that only a great increase in violence would be the result.

The ESRI report presented other, very controversial findings on attitudes in the Republic concerning Northern Irish Protestants and the IRA. Unfortunately, the conclusions of the report in these areas are highly misleading since the authors (a) failed to give information basic to an understanding of their conclusions, (b) presented statements to those interviewed which were 'slanted' in one direction, yielding a distorted view of people's real attitudes and (c) misinterpreted the data which they did present to yield an even more distorted picture (see the author, *Irish Times*, 30 October 1979).

The Northern Irish problem for the Irish, therefore, is that they find themselves, for historical reasons, engaged in a struggle with an opponent of whom they are actually fond, contesting the sovereignty of a people whom they would really rather do without. It is an internecine dispute between the heart and the head of Ireland, with Cathleen ní Houlihan putting a brave face on it.

The British-Irish Problem

Irish history is a minefield of excruciating ironies. One such irony is that a pope was the first man to send a British army into Ireland in the twelfth century. The irony is only slightly blunted by the fact that the pope in question was Hadrian IV, the one and only English pope in the history of the Catholic Church. His motive in issuing the Bull *Laudabiliter* sanctioning the invasion, proposed by King Henry II of England for domestic political reasons, was to secure the fealty of the Irish church. At the time the church in Ireland was unique among European churches in having its own organisation independent of Rome (Lebow, 1976). The admixture of politics and religion was thus an early and unwanted import to Ireland.

The British image of the Irish can be traced back to that point in time and its various modifications through history have been, to some extent, a response to the inevitable consequences, albeit sometimes unintentional, of the basis of Anglo-Irish relations which that twelfth century intervention established.

English historians from the twelfth to the nineteenth century depicted the Irish as being primitive and inferior and gave the impression that while the ordinary Irish were at least good-natured and docile, their leaders were to blame for all the troubles with which the English government had to deal (O'Farrell, 1975). To some extent, this attitude persisted through history until relatively recently. Churchill's victory broadcast on the 13 May 1945, referring to Irish neutrality during World War II, illustrates from the recent past, the traditional British view that Irish leaders do not represent the wishes of the Irish people :

'Owing to the action of the Dublin government, so much at variance with the temper and instincts of thousands of Southern Irishmen who hastened to the battle front . . . the approaches which the Southern Irish ports and airfields could easily have guarded, were closed by hostile aircraft and U-boats. . . . When I think of these days, I also think of other episodes and personalities. I think of Lieutenant-Commander Esmonde, V.C., or Lance Corporal Keneally, V.C., and Captain Fegan, V.C., and other Irish heroes whose names I could easily recite, and then I must confess that bitterness by Britain against the Irish race dies in my heart.'

Ironically, it is Northern Ireland, whose 'loyalty and friendship' Churchill contrasted in his victory speech with that of the Dublin government, on which the shadow of this historical attitude now falls. The present state of direct rule in Northern Ireland is an arguably honourable, but nonetheless a direct descendent of ancient British mistrust of Irish political leaders and of the validity of the relationship between those leaders and the people they represent.

Prior to the start of the present troubles, there was probably no significant popular British awareness of the distinction between the North and South of Ireland in any meaningful sense. The Irish were the Irish and lived over there across the water. While the Irish, through the teaching of history in schools and the general political ambience of the country, were keenly aware of the historical wrongs perpetrated by British governments, the British were largely unaware of the sins of their fathers. In

English history, Ireland has been but an occasional distraction to England's gaze towards the wider horizons of her empire.

O'Farrell (1975) compares Anglo-Irish relations to the story of the leaking roof. When storms made attention imperative, the climate was against anything other than temporary repairs; when the weather was clear, the problem could be forgotten. The comparison is apt, for the historical English view of the Irish was of an integral and useful, if occasionally troublesome, domestic fixture. They were seen as a somewhat inferior, at times very inferior, version of Englishmen. After all, they were white, usually spoke English (or at least had a go at it), lived next door and even had MPs at Westminster, if you please.

Knowledge or belief is an integral aspect of the formation and maintenance of social attitudes, although its contribution can best be understood in psychological rather than logical terms. It is rational enough that information concerning positive (or negative) characteristics of social groups should produce positive (or negative) attitudes towards those groups. The psychology of the relationship between information and attitudes, however, is, on the one hand, that we tend to select our information to suit our attitudes and, in the other, that our attitudes cloud our judgement of what constitutes reliable and relevant information. Thus purchasers of new cars tend to read only advertising features about their make and model of car partly to avoid the possibility of discovering that they have made the wrong choice (Festinger, 1964) and one tends to find relatively few Democrats attending Republican party conventions.

The closest source of information on the Irish for the people of Britain has been the Irish in their midst, working and living, chiefly in England and Wales. Typically, these have been people motivated to leave Ireland to escape poverty and unemployment or, more positively, simply to seek a better economic life in Great Britain. Popularly, they have been associated with the building trades and hard labouring jobs, which is historically reasonably accurate, although the pattern is now changing (O'Connor, 1974). The music-hall or vaudeville image of the Irishman, still prevalent to some degree, has been of a soft-hearted, simple-minded individual with too many children and too fond of drinking and fighting.

There is an element of truth in all the individual assertions

which this image contains, although these elements do not constitute a sound basis for judging the Irish in Britain generally,
much less so in Ireland. For example, the Irish are disproportionately prominent in crime statistics in England, but as
O'Connor (1974) notes (*a*) most crime is committed by males
between the ages of fifteen and forty-four in which group there
are disproportionately high numbers of Irish compared with the
native population and (*b*) the Irish are over-represented among
the urban poor, among whom the crime rate is generally high.
When one looks at crime rates in Ireland per thousand of the
population, one finds that they are much lower than rates in
England and Wales, running at approximately one-third of the
British rate between 1968 and 1976 (personal calculation from
official statistics of both countries).

However, as we have noted, attitudes have less to do with facts
than they have with the selection and interpretation of facts and,
although increasingly approximating the native population in
socio-economic status, the Irish remain the butt of popular ethnic
jokes. In October 1967, a nationwide Gallup Survey indicated
a distinct lack of enthusiasm for the Irish in Britain among the
natives. The question asked was 'Do you think that on a whole,
the country has benefited or been harmed through immigrants
coming to settle here from Ireland?' The responses were as follows : benefited, 16 per cent; harmed, 22 per cent; no difference,
46 per cent; don't know, 16 per cent. It is unlikely that paramilitary activities in Ulster and IRA activities in Britain in the
intervening years have improved that image although some
journalists, surveying the English scene for Irish newspapers,
currently detect a new respect for the achievements of the Irish
at home. For example, Mary Kenny notes a recent tendency in
the media to ignore the staple diet topics of Irish coverage, namely
the Ulster conflict and the priest-ridden nature of the Irish
Republic, in favour of more positive comment, for example on
the economic success of the Irish in recent years (*Sunday
Independent*, 31 December 1978).

As noted previously, the point of scanning these British views
of the Irish is that the British public (and, indeed, most people
in other countries) have tended to perceive Ireland geographically
rather than politically and hence lump Southern and Northern
Irish people together. Hence a knowledge of British attitudes to

the Irish generally gives a useful indicator of British attitudes to the Northern Irish in particular. We might note that while, in the past, this outlook has been an irritant to many Northern Irish Unionists, paradoxically it is now probably more of an irritant to average citizens of the Republic of Ireland and to immigrants to Britain from the Republic.

However, when it comes to attitudes towards Northern Ireland specifically in recent years, the British media have given the inevitable psychological process of selecting and interpreting facts a helping hand. To some extent, this has been as a result of government pressure but also as a result of a noticeable disparity between British professional journalistic standards in Northern Ireland and those standards elsewhere.

In general terms, it appears that the British public have been given a version of events in Ulster during the past ten years, which has favoured the British, the British Army, the British government and the Unionist party. This bias would be un-remarkable in a wartime situation, but when the conflict is between institutions in the form of the army, the police and the government and British citizens, Catholics and Protestants in Northern Ireland, then the unremarkable becomes the quite extraordinary.

There is strong evidence that British citizens have been un-justifiably killed and maimed in Ulster by members of the security forces, which is not, in the circumstances, so remarkable. How-ever, the fact that some of these incidents have never been reported in the British media is almost incredible (McCann, 1971; *Inside Story*, 1972). McCann (1971) notes that 'The real sustained and systematic distortion began when British soldiers came onto the streets. . . . As far as the British press was con-cerned the soldiers could do no wrong.' The British publication, *Inside Story*, has given examples of unreported maiming and killing by British soldiers. In one instance, an Andersonstown woman was blinded by a rubber bullet fired into her face at point-blank range for ignoring the impolitely expressed instruc-tion of a passing soldier that her window be closed. In another instance, the army, through the honesty of an individual press officer, admitted that they had, in 'confusion', shot and killed an unarmed man whom they had previously described as a gun-man. The British media declined to report either of these events.

The blame for this state of affairs is variously laid at the feet of the British Army P.R. organisation (*Inside Story*, 1972; Hoggart, 1973), the Unionist influence in the television media via top executives of BBC Northern Ireland and Ulster Television (*Inside Story*, 1972), the British government through its press officers in the Northern Ireland Office (*Fortnight*, 1973a), administrative difficulties and the now repetitive nature of Ulster news (Paxman, 1978) and journalists themselves (*Inside Story*, 1972; Hoggart, 1973). However, one fact, whose shadow falls across all of these influences, is that the version of events in any incident involving the British Army emanates primarily and almost invariably from the army itself, 'often within twenty minutes of its happening' (Hoggart, 1973).

There is a virtual ban on publishing the views of IRA leaders and this ban has been extended at times to include some priests and civil rights leaders (*Inside Story*, 1972). The onus has, therefore, been on individual journalists to pursue and examine the veracity of army reports of incidents. With notable exceptions, this responsibility has been avoided (Hoggart, 1973). Bloody Sunday was one of the few occasions when journalists were on the scene of an incident and not dependent on army accounts of what actually happened (e.g. Winchester, 1974).

The accounts of the typical modus operandi of British journalists in Northern Ireland by conscientious British journalists are not flattering. *Inside Story* (1972) paints a picture of newsmen passively waiting in the Europa Hotel, Belfast, for the inevitable telephone call from the British Army P.R. headquarters in Lisburn to supply the basis of their copy describing the latest incident in the province.

At a more general level, the biased nature of British media coverage of events in Northern Ireland is implicit in the relationship between the BBC in particular as 'an organisation within the constitution' and the British government. As Schlesinger (1978) notes, 'For broadcasting to be genuinely impartial, it would have to pose questions seriously and continuously about the persistence of British rule in one part of the United Kingdom. And this would entail consideration of the political plans of the two IRA factions.' (p. 206)

Schlesinger describes the process whereby, to avoid open and direct government censorship, the British broadcasting hierarchy followed a policy of 'responsibility' in news and current affairs coverage of Northern Ireland which started openly as support for the army against the IRA but degenerated into systematic pro-establishment distortion such that genuinely objective and analytical coverage became the exception rather than the rule.

Both Elliott (1976) and Schlesinger point out that there was a gradual drift away from analysis to a 'who, what, where and when' approach which, while enabling the media to avoid the political repercussions of questioning British policy in Ireland, has rendered events in Ireland unintelligible to the British public. As Schlesinger (1978) concludes: 'In general, broadcasting presents us with a series of decontextualised reports of violence, and fails to analyse and re-analyse the historical roots of the Irish conflict. Such an approach is largely shared by the rest of the British media, and this cannot but contribute to the dominant public view of Northern Ireland's present troubles as largely incomprehensible and irrational. It is not surprising that many see "terrorism" as the cause of the conflict there rather than as one of its symptoms.' (p. 243)

In summary therefore, the British view of the Northern Irish problem is conditioned by (*a*) historical shadows of past misunderstandings in Anglo-Irish relations, (*b*) popular and traditional attitudes towards the Irish in Britain, (*c*) British involvement in the Northern Irish conflict, (*d*) the biased media coverage of that problem and British responsibility in it and (*e*) the psychological processes which select and interpret information in the formation and maintenance of social attitudes.

Successive opinion polls over the years in Great Britain have shown that the majority feel that Britain should pull out of Ireland for good and let the Irish in Ulster get on with it. This view has had public airing in the higher echelons of the Labour and Liberal parties but both Labour and Conservative governments have resisted the temptations of such a solution in favour of the unpalatable hard slog of continued involvement. Roy Jenkins, when Home Secretary, noted in 1967 that 'despite the many attributes of the English, a peculiar talent for solving the problems of Ireland is not among them'. In the light of subsequent events, few in Great Britain, or anywhere else, would disagree with him.

In a sense, then, British public attitudes to the Northern Irish have come full circle in a decade. They have moved from regarding the Irish as a geographical nation, through the realisation that there are differences among the Irish, back to the view that they are sufficiently similar, particularly in their propensity for violence, destruction and intransigence, to justify the cessation of further British efforts to maintain the imagined differences which they perceive among themselves.

Thus for Britain, the Northern Ireland problem is that, because of the sense of duty of their government, they are unwillingly and unreasonably caught in the middle of a distasteful dispute between two groups of intransigent, belligerent Irishmen. The dispute is not of their making, except in some vague historical sense and yet they find themselves engaged in preserving as British a part of Ireland which, by the behaviour of its inhabitants is demonstrably not British and of which they would dearly love to be rid.

American Views

It is sometimes remarked in popular wit of the United States that the English own it and the Irish run it. Whatever truth that view might contain, it does illustrate an essential feature of American stances towards the Northern Irish problem. Historically, culturally and emotionally the United States has a foot in both camps and any widespread popular appeal, which supporting the perceived underdog might have had, has lost much of its naïve glamour in the sober years of self-appraisal after the Vietnam débâcle.

There is no 'American view' of the Northern Irish problem, but rather a diverse collection of views, often conflicting, often seriously misinformed, of what the problem is, who is to blame and what can be done about it. In a historical study of American views of the Irish question in the period 1919–1923, Carroll (1978) found it impossible to tackle anything other than the views of Irish-Americans and even here he found a wide diversity of opinion, even at a period when one might have inferred a greater consensus among Irish-American views than is probable today. Reflecting this diversity, the current presidential orientation is economically positive but politically neutral. However, Speaker 'Tip' O'Neill's appeal, on a visit to Ireland and Britain in April 1979, that *something* be done to ease the present stalemate, was widely misinterpreted among British politicians as indicating an anti-British stance.

As Cruise O'Brien (1978) has noted, it is probably not possible to estimate how many and how much Americans concern themselves with Ireland because Irish-Americans are not really identifiable as a population. However, as he goes on to argue, Americans with Irish interests have historically exerted profound influences on events in Ireland and that influence continues, diminished as it is.

American opinions seem to range from the staunchly Irish Republican view of history and the old country of some Irish Americans who see the IRA as justified in their campaign and, therefore, afford the organisation moral and financial support, through various hues of concern for breaches of human rights, which attract the concern of both Irish and other American politicians and commentators, to the more general blank incomprehension of, or indifference to, the entire situation expressed by most Americans.

Just as the British have tended to view Irish leaders as unrepresentative of views of Irishmen when they appear to be acting unreasonably, 'green' Irish-Americans have, in recent years, tended to view Irish leaders as unrepresentative when they appear to be acting reasonably by, for example, condemning the violence of the IRA. Indeed, as Cruise O'Brien (1978) notes, there has been a tradition of imagining that Irish-Americans, 'being free to speak in the land of the free, constitute the authentic voice of Ireland.' This atavistic and unrealistic identification of Irishness with acute anti-Britishness appears to be the trump green card which IRA leaders have successfully played in fundraising expeditions to the United States during the present troubles.

In general, the American public is relatively ignorant about Ireland, and Northern Ireland in particular. However, this does not reflect a bias in the media against coverage of Ireland. Rather it reflects the parochial nature of media coverage of news events in general and the appallingly low priority given to news analysis in American television. Commenting on the American scene from New York, Sean Cronin has written 'Serious television programmes are dying here. News documentaries on important subjects are buried at the bottom of the ratings. Television is a wasteland.' (*Irish Times*, 11 January 1979)

In the United States, one does not listen to the news but rather one watches the news show. Even the weather report is given by some bright and breezy individual who is chosen for his or her likely ratings appeal, regardless of meteorological expertise. The content tends to be consistent with the format and presentation. Short, superficial stories are the norm with foreign coverage largely confined to those with a strong American link. Thus, the Arab-Israeli dispute was given some prominence in 1978 largely because much of the drama of that conflict was enacted in Washington.

The Public Broadcasting Service, funded by government grants and public donations, and, therefore, relatively free from commercial pressures, gives greater priority to news analysis but is not popular. One PBS programme, the *McNeil/Lehrer Report* devotes thirty minutes to the analysis of one news topic per week. Unremarkable as this is by, for example, British standards, the programme is hailed in the United States as having reinvented television news. The absurdity of this notion is not lost on its presenter, Robert McNeil, who worked for four years on the BBC current affairs programme, *Panorama* (Nadel, 1977).

Simon Winchester (1974) whose coverage of Northern Ireland for the *Guardian* was distinguished, describes US media coverage of Northern Ireland as 'really rather shoddy' and their knowledge of the situation as 'little short of lamentable', granting exceptions to the *New York Times* and the *Washington Post*. Media interest in Northern Ireland has waned as a function of the lessening of violence which led Winchester to speculate that 'before too long the mythical nature of these troubles will have taken over from the factual : to judge from some of the reporting, the myths are the news already '(p. 8).

Television coverage of Northern Ireland appears, if anything, to have deteriorated since Winchester made these observations. One Californian station showed a series of short reports on Ireland during 1978, which I watched, as a rabbit does a snake. They portrayed their venture into Northern Ireland as a feat of bravery, carried out despite being warned off by the British Army. The resultant footage, needless to say, was not worth the imagined effort.

The consequence of all these phenomena is that Americans tend to be relatively ignorant of even the most basic facts of the Northern Irish situation. One American university professor with international interests with whom I spoke in 1978, was under the impression that the majority of people in Northern Ireland are Catholic. To some extent, this is probably a function of the effectiveness with which the Catholic case was publicised internationally in the early years of the present troubles but the fault lies largely with the American media in failing to inform its public sufficiently or competently about international affairs.

However, as Winchester (1974) has noted, 'ignorance provides fertile ground for sowing the seeds of propaganda', both British and Irish. IRA propaganda appears to have had some success in generating funds and support but it is more difficult to judge the effectiveness of British propaganda as its aims have been rather less tangible, namely to promote understanding of the difficulty of the British position within the situation in Northern Ireland and to justify British actions within that situation. It is therefore difficult to distinguish between support for the British position and indifference and apathy.

Pro-Catholic propaganda appears to have been responsible for generating some of the more fantastic comments about Northern Ireland, even among American politicians of international reputation. Senator Edward Kennedy in 1971 suggested that 'Britain could open its arms to any Protestants in Ulster who feel that they could not live in a United Ireland', a line of thought almost identical to that being proposed at the time by Sean MacStiofain, then leader of the Provisional IRA (Sweetman 1972, p. 157). As Cruise O'Brien (1978) has pointed out 'Americans of European descent may well discern certain flaws in such a solution . . . they are not so long established in this country [the United States] as is in Ireland . . . the community of Ulster Protestants.' One might add that such a line of thought opens up new vistas in the prospects of the American Indians.

As far as it is possible to judge the tenor of American opinion from the flimsy sources available, it seems to be one of a rather vague and uninformed sympathy for Northern Irish Catholics and a desire to see justice done in Ireland. That concern for justice in the context of a lack of information on the situation is still capable of producing strong reactions to individual events in Ulster which happen to get some publicity. Columnist Jack Anderson produced such a reaction recently with a widely syndicated diatribe on conditions in Long Kesh Prison's H-Block.

It is ironic that public opinion polls show that both the Southern Irish and British public are broadly in agreement in favouring the withdrawal of British troops from Northern Ireland and endorsing a united Ireland (Rose, McAllister and Mair, 1978). While there is no hard evidence of this, my guess would be that this would also represent the majority view of those holding opinions on the matter in the United States.

However, this apparent concurrence masks the very different reasons underlying each nation's predominant public attitudes. The British, perhaps surprisingly, appear to be most bloody-minded and irresponsible in their attitudes towards the issue. As Rose, McAllister and Mair (1978) note, 'British public opinion appears to endorse a "tough" Ulster policy for its own sake, regardless of the consequences, good, bad or nil.' (p. 27)

The notional predominant American view remains predicated on uninformed, unrealistic and long-outdated views of the Irish situation, particularly among Irish-Americans. American opinion still appears to be suffering from the imbalance caused by the very successful early civil rights propaganda campaign. This seems to be the case despite the increasing sophistication and savoir-faire of American politicians and public representatives interested in the Irish situation in recent years.

It is perhaps again surprising that the evidence suggests that the Southern Irish public are the least prejudiced, the best informed and the most hard-headed in their approach to the question of Northern Ireland, despite their endorsement of the 'old' political solutions. Unlike the British, they do not want a withdrawal of British troops and a united Ireland at any price, nor do they harbour misguided or inappropriate prejudices about their neighbours across the water, indeed quite the opposite. They do remain with a preference for a united Ireland in the ideal case but the evidence suggests that they are very keenly aware of the many problems which such a solution is likely to entail.

It must be re-emphasised at this point that the foundation on which those conclusions rest is tentative evidence and honest speculation. However it is important to try to understand public attitudes and feelings and their underlying reasons in those countries involved in the Irish problem. Most important of all, however, we must try to understand the attitudes and feelings of those within Northern Ireland and it is to this task which we now turn.

B

CHAPTER TWO

Groups and Attitudes

Social psychologists concentrate a great deal of their attention on the influences which belonging to groups has on people's behaviour. The groups to which we belong often exert a great deal of influence on how we feel about our world, what we think of it and how we behave in it. In Northern Ireland, group membership may be more than usually important for a variety of historical and political reasons. For example if we consider the large groups defined by religious affiliation, then being a Roman Catholic or a Protestant will, to a considerable extent, influence where one works, where one lives, how one votes, where one goes to school and one's attitudes to a wide range of social issues.

Obviously, Roman Catholics and Protestants in Northern Ireland are very widely affected by their religious group membership. The distinction between groups which affect members in this way (reference groups) and those which do not (membership groups) was first drawn by Newcomb (1943). Membership groups are largely devoid of reference functions. For example, membership of a table tennis club is unlikely to affect anything other than its members' appreciation of and skill at table tennis.

Three important points must be made in regard to reference groups at this point. First, it is not necessary for an individual to be a member of a group for it to act as a reference group for him. For example, the Black Civil Rights movement in the United States acted as a reference group for many young Ulster people in the initial stages of the present conflict in Northern Ireland, causing them to adopt similar tactics of protest and similar slogans. Second, although reference groups provide norms (or guidelines) for some sorts of behaviour, invariably they do not provide norms for all sorts of behaviour. Third, although a reference group is usually a group whose acceptance and approval is desired and which provides norms for one's own behaviour (a positive reference group), in some instances an individual may be influenced by a group to which he is unfavourably disposed and which may provide norms for how not to behave. For him, such a group is a negative reference group.

In the present context, a very apt example of the latter influence in action was given by Eddie McAteer, formerly a Nationalist politician for Londonderry and Leader of the Opposition at Stormont. He recounts an incident involving a Unionist politician thus: 'He was out of the chamber one day when a division was called. He was a bit flustered when he came in and asked "What way is McAteer voting?" Somebody said "For" and he said "What McAteer is for, I'm against." That epitomised the politics.' (*Irish Times*, 12 December 1977). Hence the Nationalist Party represented a negative reference group for the Unionist in question. In the particular circumstances of Northern Ireland, the concept of a negative reference group is an important one.

Finally, in regard to reference groups, it should be noted that one usually has a number of reference groups, the norms of which may or may not be in harmony. Clearly, there is a profound disparity between Christian norms and the thoughts and deeds of some of Ulster's avowed Christians on both sides of the present struggle. Dr James Scott commented on this facet of the situation that 'The peculiar tragedy of Belfast lies not in the fact that its citizens hate each other, but that they do so in the name of Christ.' (quoted in Connery 1970, p. 245)

The Ulster Protestants

Wanted—Housekeeper. Protestant (Christian preferred).

The above is the sort of curious (to the outsider) advertisement which used to appear regularly in newspaper classified columns in Northern Ireland. It would be possible to write a multi-volume text on the historical, social, economic, cultural, philosophical, educational, political and psychological implications of these five English words thus arranged. My aspirations are more modest. With the words 'Protestant' and 'Christian' transposed, the sentiments cease to be peculiarly Northern Irish, become more generally comprehensible, and are profoundly devalued in their psychological (and other) implications. We will examine these presently.

It is probably true to say that the Ulster Protestants are one of the least attractive groups in Christendom. Widely portrayed in newspapers and television around the world as a bitter and bigoted clan of power-hungry, religious fanatics, they have certainly not projected a favourable image in recent years, if they ever did. This impression is so widespread that a favourable comment leaps at the reader from the page. Bowyer Bell (1976), one of the more shrewd academic observers of the Ulster scene, makes such a comment

'. . . most Northern Protestants are not UVF assassins, frothing bigots, not evil incarnate but decent enough Christians, neighbourly, advocates of liberty, often bewildered and embittered by what appears ill-informed, self-serving attacks. . . . And, oddly enough for those swamped by the images of Paisley's preaching, the Orange parade and the institutionalised pogroms of the past, there is no greater advocate of free thinking than a thoughtful Ulster Protestant' (p. 527).

Clearly, to some extent, the wide gap between Bowyer Bell's image and the popular image reflects selective attention by the media to the 'newsworthy' and least attractive aspects of and elements among Ulster Protestants and by Bowyer Bell to the less newsworthy, less clearly categorial, but nonetheless real facets of the Ulster Protestant group. To some extent also, the popular image of Protestants in Ulster is a reflection of the success of the Catholic minority in presenting its case to the world, as argued in Chapter 1, and to the popular tendency to sympathise with the apparent underdog in any struggle. However, part of the reason why such polarised views are possible lies with the composition of the Protestant group.

Compared with other areas of the British Isles, Northern Ireland is most divided in terms of religious identification. In England, the Church of England dominates with 69 per cent of the population; in Scotland, the Church of Scotland has 68 per cent and in the Irish Republic, the Catholic Church has 95 per cent. In Wales, although the Church of England and the nonconformist churches each have 45 per cent, which has caused some minor local political problems as in the sphere of Sunday alcohol licensing laws, the problem is exclusively within the

Protestant faith and not in relation to any large non-Protestant denomination. In Northern Ireland, no denomination has a majority, but the largest single denomination is Catholic at 35 per cent, although collectively, Protestant denominations account for 63 per cent of the population.

Within the Protestant group, there are 55 denominations reported in the 1961 Northern Ireland census. The fierce independence of these groups is indicated by the fact that forty-two have less than a thousand members including two with only eleven each. The only major Protestant denominations are the Presbyterians who account for 46·9 per cent of the Protestant population (29 per cent of the total population) and the Church of Ireland which accounts for 38·3 per cent of the Protestant population (24 per cent of the total population). (Although the 1971 census obviously gives more up-to-date information on religious affiliation, its validity is reduced by the refusal of many people to answer the religious question. The 1961 data is used here on the premise that it remains a reasonable indicator of religious affiliation in Northern Ireland.)

The doctrinal differences between the Protestant denominations are by no means trivial and range from the relatively liberal Church of Ireland to the arguably monastic strictures of the Plymouth Brethren. In forms of worship, they range from the relatively 'high' Church of Ireland (by no means as high or ceremonially elaborate as some sections of its parent body, the Church of England) to the utter lay simplicity of some of the smaller sects' services, described by one Irish (Catholic) journalist recently as resembling trade union meetings rather than religious ceremonies.

The Church of Ireland, like the Roman Catholic Church, is episcopal and emphasises the importance of the clergy as interpreters of doctrine, with the final authority in the hands of the bishops. In practice, this division has caused no appreciable conflict with the philosophy of inalienable individual responsibility propounded by non-episcopal churches such as the Presbyterian Church, since the Church of Ireland has tended to be neither dogmatic nor radical. Dr Ian Paisley's much publicised theological differences with some of the Protestant churches' ecumenical negotiations, illustrates the breadth and depth of the doctrinal differences between Protestants, although his Free Presbyterian Church is neither the most dogmatic in non-ecumenical matters nor the most stringent in its demands of its members.

Church attendance is higher among Protestants in Ulster than anywhere else in the world. But although 46 per cent report attendance at least once a week and another 18 per cent at least monthly, Catholic church attendance is much higher, 33 per cent of Catholics reporting attendance more than once a week, and 62 per cent weekly (Rose, 1971). A great many Protestants in Northern Ireland rarely, if ever, attend church and it is probable, given the social desirability of church attendance in Ulster, that Rose's figures are an overestimate of church attendance among Protestants. It is precisely this local knowledge which underlies the curious advertisement presented at the beginning of this section, for the Protestant group serves only as a membership group for many Protestants rather than as a reference group providing norms of religiously appropriate behaviour, and Protestants in Northern Ireland are well aware of it.

In regard to strictly religious norms of behaviour, the Protestant group is neither very cohesive nor very homogeneous. Taking the group as a whole, the Protestant churches do not collectively serve as a positive reference group for Ulster Protestants. In order to find such positive reference functions, one must look to the subgroups within the Protestant group, namely the individual denominations. These do influence the moral affairs of their (reference) members but, as argued above, in a variety of ways.

In fact, in religious matters, it is only in relation to the Catholic Church, which serves as a negative reference group for Protestants, that any sort of cohesion in terms of norms arises within the Protestant group. Rose (1971) found in his 1968 survey that the median Protestant could find something to criticise in the Catholic Church, especially in doctrinal matters or in the question of the authority of priests. This finding must be qualified by the fact that 49 per cent of Protestants' responses to the question of which characteristics they dislike about the Roman Catholic Church, fell into the 'Nothing' or 'Don't know' categories. This ignorance of Catholicism illustrates what Wright (1973) has termed the 'autonomous' nature of the ideologies held by one community about the other in Northern Ireland, which operate to some extent independently of the facts in either case.

Rose's survey revealed that Protestant opinion was equivocal in 1968 on the issue of whether there would be any 'big changes' in relations between Protestants and Catholics in the next ten years (43 per cent 'yes', 41 per cent 'no'). This compared with a more definite 57 per cent 'yes' from Catholics. However 65 per cent of Protestants did not think that religion would ever make no difference to 'the way people feel about each other in Northern Ireland'. On the issue of ecumenical union, 40 per cent of Protestants registered explicit disapproval and 27 per cent dismissed the idea as impractical. Asked specifically about its practicality, 73 per cent of Protestants said it was impossible.

However, these are merely the statistics of antipathy. A more fundamental and interesting question is what lies behind such reactions? The answer appears to be that Protestants in Ulster have a genuine, deep-seated fear of Catholicism. For many Protestants, it seems that Catholic Churches are mysterious and forbidding places and Catholicism is a powerful, sinister and potentially engulfing creed.

The *Protestant Telegraph*, initially but no longer edited by Rev Ian Paisley, voices these fears in an unmistakable, if bizarre manner. It has identified the Roman Catholic Church as *agent provocateur* behind all sorts of international 'plots' from the assassination of John F. Kennedy, through the Common Market to the Vietnam War. In this respect, Catholicism is for some Ulster Protestants what Communism is for some Americans. Hence, it is interesting to note that on lecture tours through America's 'Bible Belt' in the late 1960s, Paisley was able to switch effortlessly from attacks on Catholicism (which would have been less intelligible to his audiences) to attacks on Communism and earn for himself a reputation in the press as a virulent anti-Communist (Abbott, 1973).

In fact, the *Protestant Telegraph* seems to see little difference between Catholicism and Communism, often treating them as functionally equivalent. Take, for example, the following reference to journalists:

... the whining multitudes of pestiferous scribbling rodents commonly known as Press reporters, newsmen and journalists. This gangrenous population, to be found in every rat hole in Fleet Street, however, are not as perilous as the typhus carriers

i.e. sub-editors and editors. These creatures are mentally flac-
cid, physically hairless, repulsive and repellent. They usually
sport thick-lensed glasses, wear six pairs of ropey sandals, are
homosexuals, kiss holy medals or carry secret membership
cards of the Communist Party. Most of them are communist-
oids, without the guts of a red-blooded Communist, or Roman
Catholics without the effrontery of a Pope Pius XII. Sometimes these anonymous editorial writers are a mixture of the
two. Spineless, brainless mongoloids. But because of it, as
maliciously perilous as vipers.' (quoted in Boulton, 1973,
p. 65)

Boulton also quotes an example in which the *Protestant
Telegraph* managed to see Catholic children in a Presbyterian
Brownie Pack as 'infiltrators', 'engaged in spreading the dogmas
of "Holy Mother Church" in the pack'. So clearly there is a fear
of Catholicism per se among some Protestants and although
most would abhor the sort of expression given to such fear in the
Protestant Telegraph's religious pornography, it is probable that
a large proportion of Protestants share, to some degree at least,
the emotions underlying it. Somewhat tangential evidence for
this assertion is given in the results of a survey by National
Opinion Polls (No. 2577) conducted on behalf of the *Belfast
Telegraph* in 1967 (at which point Paisley was more closely
involved with the *Protestant Telegraph* and the sort of sentiments it expressed). The survey showed that 32 per cent of
Protestants usually agreed with Paisley while 58 per cent usually
disagreed. My guess is that a larger percentage were in sympathy
with the fears underlying the vehement public expressions while
disagreeing with the nature and tone of the sentiments expressed.

There seems to be three major elements to the fear of Catholicism which Protestants have. First, a fear of the power of the
Catholic Church as an organisation, as revealed in such flights
of fancy as international plots and so forth. As much as anything,
this is compounded by a confusion between the Catholic Church
generally, which is, like other churches, having difficulty maintaining its influence throughout the world, and the Catholic
Church in Ireland. The Catholic Church is probably stronger
in Ireland than in any other country in the world, has a tradition of relative independence from Rome, and has had influence

in the past over political matters in the Republic of Ireland (Whyte, 1971). Rose (1971) found that 58 per cent of Protestants thought that the Catholic Church in the Republic was either powerful (39 per cent) or too powerful (19 per cent), while another 11 per cent thought it politically important.

Second, Protestants fear the power of the Catholic Church through its priests to impose its views on its members. Twenty-five per cent of Rose's (1971) Protestant respondents specifically mentioned this aspect of the Catholic Church and conversely, the most liked aspect of the Protestant churches for Protestants was 'freedom', mentioned specifically by 29 per cent. In response to the question 'How important would you say it is for members of a church to do whatever their Minister/Priest tells them?', only 30 per cent of Protestants responded 'very important' compared to 62 per cent of Catholics. Another 27 per cent of Protestants thought it 'fairly important' to obey ministers, but there is a psychological chasm between 'fairly' and 'very' in response to such a question of moral imperatives.

Protestants of all shades of opinion tend to recoil from the Catholic Church's dogmatic standpoints on contraception, divorce and, in so far as it relates to the personal safety of the mother, abortion, although divorce and abortion are not generally approved among Ulster Protestants. One particular sore point with Protestants has been the *Ne Temere Decree* of 1908, which required a written statement from both parties to a religiously mixed marriage that the children of the marriage would be brought up in the Catholic faith before the marriage could take place in a Catholic Church. This requirement has now been somewhat watered down to a statement of intent by the Catholic partner of the marriage. This stricture was felt to be particularly obnoxious, not only because of the personal strains and dilemmas which it caused and the subsequent waves of family resentment on one or both sides whatever happened, but also because it seemed from the Ulster Protestant's perspective to be an underhand way of increasing Catholic numbers at the expense of Protestants.

Finally, fear of the Roman Catholic Church takes the form of a vague, almost primitive uneasiness with a body which to the Protestants is so full of mysticism, symbolism, clandestine activity (the Vatican, convents, monasteries, retreats, separate schools)

B*

and unworldly practices such as clerical chastity, monastic silence and so forth. This is, to some extent, fuelled by ignorance, but nonetheless there is a feeling that whatever motivates, for instance, young men and women to enter holy orders and subject themselves to such sacrifices as chastity, is somehow unwholesome.

Again, the *Protestant Telegraph* voices these fears most obviously and unwittingly, running series on the infidelities of the priesthood with lurid titles such as *The Love Affairs of the Vatican*. Of nuns, it has quoted the plebeian Ulster witticism that 'The older nuns are raving, while the younger nuns are craving'. The feeling that there is something more than meets the eye in Catholicism is, however absurd and unjustified, probably well ingrained in many Protestants.

Conor Cruise O'Brien (1972) caught something of the flavour of this phenomenon in general terms in looking at differences between the North and South of Ireland. Likening the North to a 'turbulent republic of barking, snarling, yelping dogs' and the South to 'a kingdom of cats, moving on padded feet', he notes '. . . I can understand that a born dog might have nightmares about being asphyxiated under all that fur.' (p. 194)

Psychologists tend to look behind expressed attitudes to examine the functions which these attitudes serve for the individuals holding them (e.g. Smith, Bruner and White, 1956; Katz, 1960). For example, Katz (1960) proposes that four different personality functions are served by social attitudes—adjustment, value expression, knowledge and ego defence. In practice, they are not entirely separate as there is a degree of overlap among them.

In the adjustment function, the individual is expressing attitudes to maximise his social rewards and minimise his social punishments. He expresses attitudes which will gain him social approval among friends, relatives and in the community generally, and which will avoid social disapproval for him. In the particularly introverted and cocooned circumstances of Northern Irish affairs prior to the premiership of Terence O'Neill, this function represented a powerful vicious circle among some Ulster Protestants, who could express negative attitudes about Catholics, both on public occasions and in private, with impunity. O'Neill's new direction slightly tilted the scales in favour of social punishments for the public expression of such views and, in the international gaze of world opinion since the onset of the present troubles, the balance of attendant rewards and punishments has been radically altered, representing a force for change in Protestant opinion.

The value expressive function allows the individual to state who he is in terms of his personal values and self-concept. As argued above, Ulster Protestants are rather clearer on what they are not than what they are and anti-Catholic attitudes are very central to the tradition of Ulster Protestantism, having been enshrined in political and cultural tradition.

The knowledge function enables the individual to understand and structure his environment, as he perceives it. Attitudes, therefore, tend to be consistent with one's version of reality and to support and supplement it. For Ulster Protestants, therefore, given that Catholics have been perceived as second-class citizens in Northern Ireland, it makes psychological sense that they should hold negative attitudes towards them. The alternative is an uncomfortable gulf between reality and attitude which people would tend to want to avoid. Again, any rise in the actual and perceived status of the Catholic minority in the province would release forces for change in Protestant attitudes towards Catholics in Northern Ireland as the process of aligning reality with attitude takes place.

The ego-defensive function of attitudes enables individuals to avoid unpleasant truths about the world and themselves through appropriate attitudes. Thus, one finds prevalent attitudes such as 'Catholics don't want to work', when the unpleasant truths so concealed are, for example, that Catholics have often been discriminated against by major Northern Irish employers (e.g. the shipyard in Belfast, the province's largest single source of employment, which employs only a small percentage of Catholics) or that successive governments have been unable or unwilling to attract industrial investment to centres of Catholic population (e.g. in the west of Ulster). This is an example of an attitude serving an ego-defensive function in terms of avoiding an unpleasant truth about the world.

Attitudes, in their ego-defensive aspect, can also enable us to avoid looking too closely at ourselves, and prejudice can sometimes serve such a function. In Northern Ireland where, as Rose (1971) notes, there are more poor Protestants than poor Catholics, the notion that Catholics are, in various ways, inferior, serves to protect the poor Protestants from the unpleasant truth that they, also, are at the bottom of the social barrel. The mechanism by which this effect is achieved is the Freudian idea of projection, or literally 'throwing out' onto others those aspects of our own behaviour or situation which we do not wish to acknowledge as really ours.

We have noted in reference to the *Protestant Telegraph* the tendency to ascribe somewhat esoteric sexual proclivities to the Catholic clergy and nuns. A more mundane and common assertion of Catholic sexual proclivity is that they 'breed like rabbits'. Although this also reflects attitudes to the Catholic dogma on contraception, it probably also reflects to some extent, a projection of sexual fantasy on the part of the Protestants in Northern Ireland. Ulster folk are typically old-fashioned in their attitudes to sex, especially working class people, and the attendant repression of sexual impulses and inhibitions on frank and open discussion of sex provide ideal conditions for the projection of sexual fantasies onto the minority. Of course, the ecologically ideal way of utilising this function, as the *Protestant Telegraph* has discovered, is to concoct an unholy brew of sexual fantasy and religious criticism.

So far, we have restricted the discussion to the Protestant view of Catholics as Catholics. Quite another issue is the Protestant view of Catholics as people. Although the sort of attitude one often hears expressed about Catholics as Catholics would lead one to believe that Protestants are incapable of viewing their Catholic neighbours as people, this is not so. Colloquially, the distinction is heralded by a phrase such as 'well, he's a Catholic but . . .' or a favourable comment about a Catholic as a person is qualified in retrospect by a phrase such as '. . . even though she's a Catholic'.

In 1968, immediately prior to the present troubles, Rose (1971) found that 67 per cent of Protestants thought that Catholics were 'about the same' as people of their own religion while only 28 per cent thought that they were 'much different'. The equivalent figures for Catholic respondents in regard to Protestants were 81 per cent 'about the same' and only 14 per cent 'much different'. Presented boldly in this way, the figures seem to indicate that Catholics have a more egalitarian outlook. But one important point must be kept in mind: the cultural tradition among Catholics is to regard all of the inhabitants of Ireland as one people, whereas the Protestant tradition is to view the Protestant inhabitants of Northern Ireland as culturally and politically separate. Thus, the fact that such a clear majority of Protestants regarded Catholics as 'about the same as' themselves in 1968 is indicative of a basic egalitarianism at that time, transcending cultural and political traditions. But how have the events of the intervening years affected these attitudes? A study published in 1977 by O'Donnell may give us an insight into this question. It is worthwhile spending a little longer than usual in examining the strengths and weaknesses of O'Donnell's study since it provides a unique post-trouble source of comparison with Rose's pre-trouble data and affords us some means of gauging the effects of the intervening years of conflict on inter-group attitudes in Northern Ireland.

The study in question was originally presented as a Ph.D. thesis in the University of Southern California in December 1975. The date is important because the author omits to tell us when the study was actually carried out, which leaves us to guess that it was conducted during the latter part of 1974 and possibly early 1975, but at least at a time when enough had happened in Northern Ireland to call into question the current validity of Rose's 1968 data on Protestant views of Catholics and vice-versa.

O'Donnell's investigation asked respondents of each religion four basic questions. Protestants were asked: 1. How would you describe the Protestants of Northern Ireland? 2. How would you describe the Roman Catholics of Northern Ireland? 3. How do you think the Roman Catholics of Northern Ireland would describe themselves? 4. How do you think the Roman Catholics would describe the Protestants of Northern Ireland? Catholics were asked questions 1 and 2 and conversely worded versions of questions 3 and 4.

O'Donnell particularly wished to examine stereotypes in Northern Ireland. Stereotypes are generalised and simplified 'working models' of others which vary in their accuracy. We do not have stereotypes of our close friends and relatives because we have enough information about each of them to react towards each one as an individual. Stereotypes arise in relation to groups of which our information is patchy and scant. They can be positive or 'good' models or negative, 'bad' models irrespective of how accurate they actually are. Young boys have positive stereotypes of train drivers, pilots and cowboys. Adults frequently have negative stereotypes of people of a different ethnic origin or even of different sex. Most commonly, those holding these stereotypes know little about the people behind the stereotypes. Stereotypes help us to order and categorise our social environment. Vinacke (1957) notes that it is the content of stereotypes and how they are used, rather than the mere fact of their use, that constitutes their legitimate consideration as an aspect of prejudice.

O'Donnell's technique was to use a word-list of one hundred adjectives from which his respondents were invited to choose in their descriptions. Initially, three hundred words and expressions were 'collected' in various environments in Northern Ireland, and these were reduced to two hundred 'by excising exact synonyms and vulgarities'. Six well-educated 'judges' were individually asked to reduce these two hundred terms to one hundred of the most commonly used terms in Northern Ireland and a master list of one hundred terms was compiled from the consensus among the resultant lists. It is not altogether clear how the elimination of vulgarities, at least in the literal sense of the word, and the utilisation of six judges each of whom 'held at least a Master's university degree' could theoretically produce the most valid list of commonly used terms in Northern Ireland. However, the resultant selection is quite comprehensive although there are some very unfortunate omissions.

It is primarily in regard to the method by which O'Donnell's subjects were chosen that one has certain reservations about his data. They were divided by sex, age, location in the province, religious affiliation and socio-economic background and were obtained in eighty-four groups of twenty. Each group filled a certain set of criteria within the above framework and there was a total of 1,680 subjects.

The problem arises principally in regard to the socio-economic background distinction drawn by O'Donnell. He classified subjects as either working class or middle class, a perfectly normal procedure usually. Unfortunately, however, the Northern Irish are peculiar in regard to their class attachments. Rose (1971) found that 44 per cent of his Northern Irish respondents thought of themselves as middle class, compared to 22 per cent of Scottish respondents and 28 per cent of English respondents in a 1964

Gallup poll. Also, 22 per cent of Rose's respondents did not place themselves in any class compared to 7 per cent of such people in Scotland and 6 per cent in England in the Gallup poll.

It is conceivable that a comparison of working and middle class attitudes based on subjective assessment in Northern Ireland would yield a different picture to such a comparison based on a more objective system such as the Registrar-General's Classification of Occupations. There is, at present, no data bearing on this issue. The issue could be held in abeyance if the author had decided on one system or the other and then assiduously stuck to it. We would then have been in a position to evaluate his social class data on the premises chosen and to re-evaluate them in the light of subsequent research findings on the differences, if any, produced by the two classification systems.

Regrettably, O'Donnell does not make clear precisely which criteria his study used and this difficulty is exacerbated by the fact that the author neither met nor chose any of his subjects personally, which, at least, would have guaranteed some consistency. In fact, the subjects were chosen by eighty-four different 'contacts', each one choosing a group of twenty subjects according to the specifications of the author in regard to the variables mentioned above. It is reasonable to assume, in view of the author's vagueness on this point, that a considerable amount of diversity may have arisen as to precisely who should be categorised as working or middle class and that one or both groups may yield a distorted picture of class-related stereotypes in Northern Ireland. For example, it seems plausible that O'Donnell's contacts may have played safe by choosing people who were 'very obviously' working class or middle class and thereby failed to feed into the study the full range of opinions which are held in both classes. It may be, in fact, that O'Donnell's subjects reflect his contacts' diverse stereotypes of what sorts of people belong in the working and middle classes.

However, despite these particular reservations, there is considerable value in O'Donnell's data, especially, with regard to the overall opinions of one side about the other. It is not easy to do research of this kind anywhere, least of all in Northern Ireland at present and most of the criticisms presented here concern methods by which O'Donnell has attempted to circumvent research difficulties in the field. It is more or less a fact of academic life that field research inevitably entails compromise with methodological purity.

The most striking finding that O'Donnell's work reveals is that, despite what happened between Rose's survey in 1968 and O'Donnell's investigation, the Protestant view of Catholics has remained remarkably stable and benign, all things considered. The term used most often by Protestants to describe Catholics was 'ordinary people' followed by 'Irish'. The ten most frequently used terms also included items of religious criticism ('priest-ridden', 'breed like rabbits', 'brainwashed'), items of political affiliation ('Republican', 'Nationalistic'), and items of general comment ('bitter', 'superstitious', 'not bad').

Protestants think that Catholics would describe them as 'power holders', 'British', 'Orangemen' and 'bigoted' and to a lesser extent that they would feel that Protestants are 'enemies', 'murderers', 'bitter', 'narrow-minded' and 'no surrender', which is a substantially accurate picture of how Catholics actually do see Protestants as we shall see later.

Protestants see themselves most unanimously as 'British', somewhat less so, 'loyalist' and then as 'ordinary people', 'determined', 'decent', 'fine people', 'industrious', 'Orangemen', 'conservative' and 'power-holders' in that order.

The combination of the 'real' stereotypes that Protestants have of Catholics and Protestants and the 'supposed' sterotypes, which they think Catholics have of them, seems to indicate that Protestants see themselves in an impossible situation. They are ordinary, decent people, who want to hold onto their British identity and yet their Catholic neighbours, who are also ordinary people and not bad, because they are priest-ridden and brainwashed into their Republican ways see them as power-holding, bigoted murderers.

In summary, the arguments presented here point to the fact that the central sticking point of the Protestants' attitudes toward the Catholic minority is religious and is maintained by an underlying psychological matrix of misconceptions and fears about Catholicism, its organisation and its power. Most Protestant criticisms of Catholics have something to do with religion and, to a lesser extent, politics, while maintaining a central attitude of Catholics as ordinary people. Wright's (1973) thoughtful analysis of Protestant ideology arrived at much the same point in emphasising the importance of the religious issue and its ramifications. Nelson (1975), in considering Protestant ideology, also emphasises that the central problem for Protestants is the Roman Catholic Church and rightly dismisses the notion that Ulster Protestant views are in any meaningful sense 'racist' as, for example, de Paor (1970) initially suggested.

This is not to argue that Protestant antipathies toward Catholicism and (hence) Catholics have not been manipulated by political leaders, as so often happens in genuine racial conflicts. Nor is it to argue that when one looks at the separate but related issue of Protestant attitudes towards a united Ireland that fear of the Catholic Church is the exclusive issue. As O'Donnell's (1977) data has shown, the question of British identity is still of great importance and it is undoubtedly true that Gaelic culture in the form of sport, language and so forth is alien to many Protestants (Gibson, 1971).

Equally, although economic differences between the North and the South of Ireland have decreased considerably in recent years, British social welfare payments still clearly favour the poor in Northern Ireland (Gibson, 1974). This difference would tend to reinforce anti-united Ireland views particularly among poor Protestants, whose views on the matter tend to be strongest in any case. However, the argument here is that the most psychologically deep-seated reason why Protestants in Northern Ireland are resistant to a united Ireland is that they fear the Catholic Church.

Two sub-groups, which are commonly thought to exert or to have exerted great influence over Protestants, are the Orange Order and the Unionist Party. We shall now endeavour to examine the position of these subgroups in the overall structure of the Protestant group.

The Orange Order

It has been argued above that the Protestant denominations do not collectively serve any substantial positive reference function for Protestants in religious matters. However, they do have a collective positive reference group in the Orange Order, although it is a rather weaker one than is often supposed. It is not appropriate here to give even a brief introduction to the history of the Orange Order since that is difficult to do and I would prefer to leave the reader in ignorance rather than in error. Gray's (1972) account of the Orange Order is brief, up-to-date and objective and I have relied substantially on his analysis in this dicussion.

The Orange Order is a Masonic-type organisation with explicit religious and political objectives. In religious terms it stands for good, Protestant, clean living, fundamental sabbatarianism and most importantly, vehement opposition to the Roman Catholic Church. However, it formally requires that each member be 'ever abstaining from all uncharitable words, actions or sentiments towards his Roman Catholic brethren' and professedly denies to membership 'persons whom an intolerant spirit leads to persecute, injure or upbraid any man on account of his religious opinions'. Gray (1972) makes the fair point that '. . . there is a double-think running right through the fabric of the Orange Institution which blinds its members to the fact that their written aims, objects and aspirations bear little relationship to the actions of some, at any rate, of their members.' (p. 195) More succinctly, Barritt and Booth (1972) observe that 'Many would think this an aim more honoured in the breach than in the observance.' (p. 36)

In political terms, the Order is pledged to 'support and maintain the Laws and Constitution of the United Kingdom, and the succession to the throne in Her Majesty's illustrious house, being Protestant'. Members, on joining the order are also required to support 'Orange and Protestant candidates only, and in nowise refrain from voting, remembering our motto "He who is not with us is against us" '. In practice, this has meant the support of Unionist Party candidates. The Unionist Party Council reserved approximately one-fifth of its seats for Orange delegates and the Order has seats on many local constituency associations.

The lodges, of which there are approximately 2,000, meet about once a month and attendance is poor for most of the year, picking up just before the 12 July, when details of the annual parades and celebrations are being discussed. Business at these meetings, although opponents make a great fuss about their secrecy, is usually humdrum and involves such matters as contributions to local charities and the sort of sandwiches the lodge should organise for its members' picnic on the 12 July. The Order claims 100,000 members, although it also claims to keep no details of membership and some of its officials think the figure of 100,000 more appropriate to Ireland as a whole. (There are some lodges in the Republic of Ireland.) Rose (1971) estimates the number at about 90,000 or approximately one-third of Protestant men.

The Orange Order emphasises relatively uncontroversial issues among Ulster Protestants: clean living, loyalty to the throne as distinct from any particular Westminster Party, opposition to Roman Catholicism and the maintenance of the constitutional position of Northern Ireland. It is largely a rural organisation, only 15 per cent of its members coming from Belfast (Rose, 1971) and appears to attract neither the well-educated young nor the professional middle classes (Gray, 1972; Barritt and Booth, 1972). For many, and this is particularly true in rural areas, it serves an important social function and it is undoubtedly true that some join it primarily for its social aspects, its somewhat adolescent secrecy rituals and elaborate nomenclature, and the pageantry, colour and excitement of its public demonstrations, rather than because of any burning desire to cock-a-snook at the local Catholics. Many also join it as a family tradition ('The sash my father wore').

The Orange Order has a relatively clear-cut image in Ulster, only two characteristics in Rose's survey being widely noted. Forty-seven per cent of respondents saw it as standing for the Protestant religion and 26 per cent saw it as standing for the maintenance of a Protestant and Unionist regime. Thirty-six per cent of Protestants strongly approved of the Order in the Loyalty survey (Rose, 1971) while only 5 per cent strongly disapproved. However, this leaves 59 per cent in other, rather nebulous categories such as 'somewhat approve', 'mixed views', 'somewhat disapprove' and 'no opinion/don't know'.

Overall, it is probably fair to conclude that the Orange Order serves as a positive reference group for about one-third of Protestant men in Northern Ireland. For the rest, while only a small proportion unequivocally disapprove of it, there are varying degrees of ambivalence towards it. Among Protestants, these equivocal views probably range from those who see it as a necessary evil, like the public hangman, to pressurise the government to stand firm on the constitutional issue, to those who see it as a somewhat anachronistic and silly organisation which, nonetheless, adds a touch of colour and tradition to Ulster life. It is conceivable that quite a few Catholics would fall into the latter category also, especially in times of relative calm in the province, for in Rose's 1968 survey, before the present troubles began, only 34 per cent of Catholics strongly disapproved of the Order's influence on life in Northern Ireland.

The Unionist Party

Traditionally, Protestants in Ulster have voted for the Unionist Party. There are exceptions; for example, the Shankill Road district of Belfast, where strong loyalism and poverty curiously combine, has a history of voting for socialist-oriented candidates, either Northern Ireland Labour Party candidates or left-wing Unofficial or Official Unionists (Wright, 1973).

Traditional Unionism, before the current disintegration into various splinter parties, was a remarkably uninfluential force on Protestants in Ulster. Its reference function for its group members was virtually nil, for it was a one-issue party, standing only for the constitutional link with Great Britain and consequent separation from the Republic of Ireland. But since the Orange Order had stood for loyalty to the Crown, and hence, de facto after 1921, separation from the Republic of Ireland, Unionism had nothing unique to offer its followers in terms of reference functions. In fact, Unionist activists, including politicians and party workers, merely fulfilled a role for the Protestant group in looking after their constitutional interests and running the country in their best interests. Indeed, the lack of distinction between the Unionist Party and the people it represented is evident from the fact that the Ulster Covenant, pledging a determination to resist Home Rule, was signed on the 28 September 1912 by almost half a million Protestants, a large majority of the entire adult Protestant population.

Putting this another way, the Unionist Party had no philosophy to offer to Protestants. A reference group influences its members over a wide range of attitudes and outlooks as, for example, the Labour Party in Britain or the Republican Party in the United States. In Ulster, what reference function there was operated in the opposite direction, with the Unionist Party being more often swayed by the Orange Order than vice-versa. And when O'Neill began to operate outside the role expectations of a Unionist group leader and invest reference functions in the Unionist

Party by his actions and statements, many Protestants began to resist and resent his presumption.

From what has been argued above, it would be wrong to say that Protestants found themselves with conflicting group norms under O'Neill's premiership (Protestant *vs* Unionist or Protestant and Orange *vs* Unionist). Rather they found that the groups to which they belonged were very limited in their cohesion, largely because their reference functions covered too narrow a band of relevant issues and offered prescriptions in too limited a range of circumstances. Only if the Catholic minority were prepared to continue fulfilling their role as passive and silent opponents; only if the British government was prepared to continue to ignore Ulster; only if the eyes of the world remained averted from Ulster affairs; only if the Protestants *en masse* continued to consider what they were against to the exclusion of what they were for, could the Protestant group's fragile cohesion continue to bind them together. The amazing thing is that all these conditions remained fulfilled for so long.

It is only since the disintegration of the Unionist Party that Unionism has begun to take on any reference functions at all. There are now several Unionist parties among which Protestants can choose and which, therefore, by choosing become reference groups for them. There is also the middle-of-the-road Alliance Party (although the road in question is rarely sullied by other than dainty, well-shod middle class feet) and the small and weak Northern Ireland Labour Party.

Thus in terms of group psychology, the Ulster situation is, potentially, more mobile than it has been at any time in its recent history for, although the Unionist parties have been drawn together under the umbrella of the United Ulster Unionist Council (UUUC), in some important respects their aims and ultimate sanctions are incompatible. Some advocate closer integration with Westminster, whilst others stress the need for devolved government in Northern Ireland. Some are prepared to share power with politicians whose ultimate aim is a United Ireland, while this is out of the question for others. Some demur to the ultimate authority of the British government while others are not above challenging that authority on the streets.

They are united only in their resistance to the idea of a United Ireland. Their leaders are frequently and publicly at odds with each other and it is likely that, in a working political situation, their differences would become more rather than less problematical, since, in the present political vacuum of direct rule, their disagreements are theoretical, camouflaged and easily glossed over, temporarily at least, in a desire to present a united front to their political masters at Westminster.

The Catholics

In terms of religion, at least, Northern Ireland's Catholics are very much more homogenous and cohesive than their Protestant counterparts and present a much simpler psychological picture. Although there are wide variations in the degree to which individual Catholics practise and believe what the Catholic Church teaches and expects, there is no equivalent of the myriad denominations to which Protestantism gives rise and the range and extent of individual variation in practice and belief is probably less than in any of the major Protestant denominations.

Church attendance once per week or more was reported by 95 per cent of Rose's Catholic respondents, roughly double the weekly attendance figures for Protestants. Catholics are relatively happy to accept the authority of their church as indicated by the fact that 62 per cent thought it 'very important' to do 'whatever their Minister/Priest tells them', roughly double the number of Protestants who so responded. In contrast to the Protestants, therefore, the Catholics have a strong positive reference group in their church.

Also in contrast to the Protestants, the Catholics do not see their counterparts' churches as a negative reference group. Sixty per cent of Catholics thought that religious unity between the Protestant and Catholic Churches was a good idea, compared to 19 per cent of Protestants. Barritt and Booth (1972) state simply that 'Catholics . . . do not fear the Protestant religion' (p. 2). Cruise O'Brien (1972), however, perceives that Catholics have a condescending attitude to Protestantism, recalling his typical youthful impression that '. . . Protestantism . . . was founded by Henry VIII in order to have eight wives' (p. 168). My own impression is that Cruise O'Brien is probably nearer the mark in this respect and that lay Catholics have no great objection to ecumenism since they do not take Protestantism seriously enough to regard it as a potential threat.

Rose (1971) found that his Catholic respondents, when asked what they liked about the Protestant churches, indicated a smattering of approval for a variety of characteristics but the only substantial category endorsement was 'don't know', 50 per cent so indicating. Similarly, when asked what they disliked about Protestant churches, 61 per cent responded 'nothing' and a further 22 per cent responded in the 'don't know' category. Clearly, therefore, Protestantism per se is not a serious issue among Catholics.

In 1968, Rose found that 81 per cent of Catholics thought that Protestants were 'about the same' as Catholics and only 14 per cent thought that they were 'much different'. O'Donnell's (1977) data of approximately 1974 indicate that Catholics overwhelmingly thought of Protestants as power-holders, and then bigoted, loyalist, Orangemen, British, bitter, ordinary people, brainwashed, determined and murderers.

Clearly, the most fearsome of these terms is 'murderers'. Looking at O'Donnell's analysis of the data by sex, location and social class (bearing in mind the previously expressed doubts about this classification), it would appear that this response is most common among Belfast working class women. It does not appear in the ten most frequent responses for middle class respondents, male respondents or all respondents in Londonderry or Enniskillen (the other two locations from which subjects were drawn). This presumably reflects sex differences in attitudes towards violence overlaid on the effects of the random assassination campaign conducted by Protestant paramilitary groups, with Belfast working class males as the most frequent target (Dillon and Lehane, 1973).

Much the most frequently used term in Catholic descriptions of Protestants in O'Donnell's study is 'power-holders', a reference to their political propensities. Other frequently used terms were 'loyalist', 'Orangemen', 'British' and 'brainwashed', all references to political influences and predilections (since there is no specifically religious term included among the most frequently used terms, there is no obvious alternative 'brainwashing' agent for Protestant political machinery).

So it seems that for Catholics, there is no real attitudinal or psychological problem associated with Protestantism but rather objections centre around Protestant attitudes to politics. There does not appear to be any underlying labyrinth of psychological fears supporting Catholic attitudes to Protestants. This interpretation is consistent with the fact that between the time of Rose's survey and the time of O'Donnell's survey, Catholic attitudes to Protestants appear to have deteriorated in response to the events of the intervening years, while Protestant attitudes to Catholics have remained more stable, being more deeply rooted psychologically.

In political terms, the most binding issue on the Catholic group is its desire for Irish unity. However, Catholics are as divided about the sort of United Ireland they would like as Protestants are about the sort of Northern Ireland they would like to see emerge from the present conflict. The Nationalist Party until the present troubles the largest opposition party, was, like the Unionist Party, a one-issue outfit but with no organisation, no party headquarters and, until May 1966, no annual party conference. The current heirs to the Nationalist allegiance, the Social, Democratic and Labour Party (SDLP), although nominally a socialist party, is internally split on the issue of socialism among other things (McAllister, 1977). It is prepared to work within United Kingdom and Ulster institutions but only under certain conditions, currently that any new Ulster assembly should have a power-sharing arrangement guaranteeing them government office. But, in fact, the SDLP is only unanimously and wholeheartedly behind a united Ireland.

Once again, however, the political pursuit of a united Ireland is only a role assigned to Nationalist and SDLP politicians by the members of the Catholic group. Until the unanticipated carve-up of the country by the British government, Ireland was politically united under the United Kingdom. The majority of Catholics in the Six Counties thus wrenched away from their fellow countrymen wanted a united Ireland before, during and after partition and their politicians were merely elected to make that clear. The gestural significance of their election was underlined by the fact that they were, in the past, sometimes elected to both Westminster and Stormont parliaments on the express understanding that they had no intention of attending these institutions. On occasion, they have been elected when such attendance was physically impossible since they were imprisoned or interned.

The most recent evidence available at the time of writing on Catholic political attitudes in Northern Ireland is from an unpublished study by Moxon-Browne (1979), some details of which have been published in a recent Economic and Social Research Institute report (Davis and Sinnott, 1979). This data suggests the possibility of a shift in Catholic opinion since O'Donnell's study.

Moxon-Browne surveyed a sample of 1277 Northern Irish people, 825 Protestants and 402 Catholics, in the period July to September 1978. He found that almost half of the Catholic sample disagreed with the suggestion that the British government should declare its intention to withdraw 'whether the majority agrees or not', although 64 per cent agreed that the British government should announce its intention to withdraw at a fixed date in the future. In addition, 64 per cent of the Catholic sample disagreed with the suggestion that British withdrawal without consent would lead to a negotiated settlement and 67 per cent envisioned such a withdrawal leading to a great increase in violence.

On the issue of the IRA, Moxon-Browne found that 61 per cent of Catholics thought that the Irish government should take a tougher line with them, although 55 per cent disagreed with the statement that 'The Irish government is not doing its best to ensure that the IRA is unable to operate from the Republic's side of the Border'. Sixty-four per cent of Catholics interviewed thought that the Irish government should agree to the extradition to Northern Ireland or Britain of people accused of political crimes.

In terms of political solutions, almost half of the Catholics in Moxon-Browne's study (48 per cent) thought that, ideals apart, the most workable and acceptable solution to the Northern Irish problem was for Northern Ireland to remain part of the United Kingdom, either with a devolved, power-sharing government (39 per cent) or under direct rule (9 per cent). This compared to 39 per cent support for a united Ireland, either under one government (25 per cent) or under a federal arrangement (14 per cent).

These data indicate a mellowing of Catholic opinion towards Protestant political outlook, consistent with the interpretation of the basis of Catholic antipathy toward the Protestant group put

forward above. They do not suggest that Catholics in Northern
Ireland have abandoned forever their aspirations for a united
Ireland or that they have discovered a new love for the British.
Rather it appears that a more pragmatic philosophy currently
prevails, possibly comprising such elements as the unacceptability
of continued violence, disillusionment with the Dublin government and a hard-headed appreciation of the economic advan-
tages of remaining within the United Kingdom (Conor O'Clery,
Irish Times, 23 October 1979).

The Catholic group does, nonetheless, have two reference
groups which have tended to direct its political aspirations,
namely the Gaelic Athletic Association (GAA) and the Catholic
Church. The GAA, which was founded as part of the Nationalist
movement in Ireland, has historically been the largest Repub-
lican-oriented organisation in Ulster (Rose, 1976). It organises
and promotes Gaelic sports throughout Ireland and has tended
to be a divisive influence in Ulster since, prior to 1970, it forbade
its members to play 'English' games such as rugby, cricket and
soccer, the games which Protestants tended to play. Its primary
influence has been to promote the sporting and cultural aspects
of Gaelic nationality and involve its members, through sport, in
the tradition of Gaelic nationalism.

Although the Catholic Church in Ireland rarely expresses
political views through its hierarchy except on issues in which it
is involved anyway (e.g. education and medical care), individual
Catholic clergymen, drawn as they tend to be from the local
community, have political opinions closely aligned with those
of their flock. They tend to be anti-Unionist and pro-united
Ireland (Fahy, 1971; Roche, Birrell and Greer, 1975). Hence,
even in the absence of specific public expressions of opinion by
the hierarchy, the Catholic Church tends to act as a reference
group in political aspirations also, as its members view it through
their local priests.

Although the Catholic community nominally has a counter-
part to the Orange Order in the Ancient Order of Hibernians,
functionally this is not the case. According to Rose's (1971)
survey, membership is only 2·6 per cent of the population and
Catholics and Protestants alike are largely ignorant of the
organisation. Sixty-nine per cent of Catholics and 71 per cent
of Protestants said they did not know what the organisation

stood for. Also 48 per cent of Catholics and 54 per cent of Protestants offered no opinion when asked if they approved of the influence of the organisation on life in Northern Ireland, presumably indicating that it has little or no influence.

In looking, therefore, at the groups to which Catholics and Protestants respectively belong and the current state of mutual attitudes between the two communities, it seems to be the case that two distinct and quite separate problems exist. For Protestants, their differences with Catholics are primarily religious with political differences being consequent on the religious issue. It seems to be the case that Protestants see Catholics' political aspirations as inevitable given the nature of their religion and past history. Protestants object primarily to Catholics as Catholics but not as people.

On the other hand, Catholics' current objections to Protestants concern not their religion, but their political outlook and way of doing things. However this political outlook is not imposed upon Protestants, but rather is the result of their own preferences. The term 'power-holders' connotes much more personal choice and predilection than terms such as 'Irish', 'priest-ridden' or 'Nationalistic' used by Protestants to describe Catholics. In other words, for the present at least, to some extent Catholics object primarily to Protestants as people and not as Protestants.

To further explore the dynamics of this relationship, let us consider the groups to which each side can claim technical, if not emotional membership. We have used the terms 'group' and 'subgroup' up to this point. In the following section, I will use the term 'supergroup' to indicate larger, combined groups such as the Irish or the British.

To what extent do the people of Northern Ireland, notwithstanding the group allegiances discussed above, regard themselves as collectively forming a group which is distinct from other groups? It was argued in Chapter One that both the British and the Irish in the Republic of Ireland see the Northern Irish collectively as different from themselves, in practice if not in theory.

The terms 'Irish', 'Ulster' and 'British', because of their political and historical significance, tend to have emotional connotations which make people in Northern Ireland either unduly resistant or unduly attached to them as labels, depending on their point of view. Ulster Protestants, because of the recent and fragile political nature of their province, are particularly prone to this effect and are inclined to be more strong in their attachment to the labels 'British' and 'Ulster' than Catholics are to the label 'Irish', indicating, as Rose (1971) points out, a defensive reaction to their uncertainty about their allegiances.

Perhaps we should briefly examine the de facto position about the appropriateness of these labels. Until partition, all of those native to Ireland were Irish and British, just as today, the natives of Scotland are Scottish and British. There were, of course, regional attachments and pride just as those living today in Northumberland and Durham in England see themselves as distinct in habits and outlook from Londoners or people in California see themselves as distinct from New Yorkers.

After partition, the inhabitants of Ulster were technically British but the particular 'home' label was difficult. Technically it was 'Northern Irish' since the name given to the newly defined portion of the United Kingdom was Northern Ireland. Therefore, even in a technical sense, the inhabitants were described as 'Irish', albeit qualified by the adjective 'Northern'. But 'Irish' was also the label unarguably appropriate to the inhabitants of the new Republic of Ireland whom the Protestants of Northern Ireland were so keen to keep at arm's length in the traumatic and anxious early days of Northern Ireland. It was also the label to which the Catholics of Northern Ireland were attached, again with scarcely arguable justification. The Catholics were resistant to the label 'British' on the very reasonable grounds that the British, after several hundred years of exploitation and neglect, had divided their country as a parting shot.

The home label which was adopted and promoted by the new government of Northern Ireland was 'Ulster', although this was a partition of the facts, so to speak. In the 1885 Westminster general election, fought in Ireland almost exclusively on the Home Rule issue the nine counties of Ulster returned seventeen members opposed to Home Rule and sixteen members in favour of it (de Paor, 1970). But the fight against Home Rule was fought in Ulster, and inhabitants of Northern Ireland are technically, as well as by choice in the case of Protestants, Ulstermen. But so are the inhabitants of the 'lost counties' of Donegal, Cavan and

Monaghan in the Republic of Ireland. Catholics, however, tend to have a resistance to the 'Ulster' label because of its associations with partition and Unionism.

Some evidence for these observations has been provided by Rose (1971) who found that 39 per cent of Protestants think of themselves as British, 32 per cent as Ulstermen and 20 per cent as Irishmen. Seventy-six per cent of Catholics thought of themselves as Irish, 15 per cent as British and only 5 per cent as Ulstermen. Catholics in 1968, therefore, appeared to be particularly resistant to the Ulster label to the extent that three times as many preferred the British label. Rose also found that attachment to the British and Ulster labels tended to be strong among Protestants (no doubt because of uncertainty about their actual identity) whereas of Catholics and Protestants who regarded themselves as Irish, only approximately 28 per cent felt strong identification, indicating a more easy and natural alignment of label and actuality.

One might surmise that the proportions in these categories has changed somewhat in the ensuing years of violence and upheaval, with the British identification lower among Catholics and possibly higher among Protestants as they see their constitutional position threatened. O'Donnell's more recent study of stereotypes in Northern Ireland indicates that Protestants still describe themselves more often as 'British' than anything else and that Catholics describe themselves more often as 'Irish' than anything else. Unfortunately, neither the term 'Ulsterman' nor 'Northern Irish' was included in the list from which O'Donnell's respondents could choose in their descriptions and therefore the study provides us with no means of telling how either side relates more recently to these important labels in relation to their reactions to the labels 'British' and 'Irish'.

There is however, among Ulster Protestants, a reasonably general, clandestine affection for the Irish label and a willingness to acknowledge, under certain circumstances, that the label is appropriate to them. This is particularly true of the Ulster Protestant outside Ireland where people have, until the onset of the present troubles, made no distinction between the Southern and Northern Irish and greeted attempts to differentiate the two usually with a sort of tolerant, bemused incomprehension. Although, in some respects, this ignorance of the Irish situation was (and is) a cross which touchier Protestants have had to bear, there are times when it is not much of a burden.

It is probably true that most Protestants in Ulster are willing to bask in any praise of the Irish and their characteristics generally. There was widespread pride in Northern Ireland, among both Catholics and Protestants, at John F. Kennedy's election and presidency in the United States (Gray, 1966) and a genuine and widespread sadness on his death. Conversely, when the Irish generally are under some form of attack, it is difficult for the Protestant Ulsterman to entirely dissociate himself from the force of the attack because of his curiously partial attachments and because of his knowledge that outsiders neither know nor care about differences among the Irish. The 'Irish' label is, therefore, by no means devoid of cohesive or reference properties, especially in regard to forces both positive and negative (but more particularly positive), in the outside world.

Equally, it is true that the Northern Irish supergroup is not without reference functions for Northern Irish Catholics. Ulster Catholics do tend to take a quiet pride in the Ulsterman's image of hard worker and '. . . are inclined to look upon Irishmen below the border as a feckless lot of layabouts.' (Connery, 1970, p. 250). Interestingly, this stereotype of the Southern Irish is also held by (non-British) foreign visitors to Ireland who tend, according to a recent study, to view the Irish in the Republic as comparatively lazy and unambitious (Concannon O'Brien, 1979). In contrast to this image, Miller (1978), in a survey and analysis of the attitudes to work of over 2,400 Catholics and Protestants in Northern Ireland, found distinctly favourable attitudes and quite remarkably similar outlooks between Catholics and Protestants in their evaluation of the moral, personal and intrinsic benefits of work. The Protestant ethic is alive and well and living in the Falls Road!

Again, there are also external forces wielding potentially cohesive influences on the Northern Irish label. The tendency, described in Chapter One, for both the British public and the Southern Irish public to tar all of the inhabitants of Northern Ireland with the same brush as a result of the prolonged and unreasonable nature of the present conflict, is conducive of a self-perception among Ulster Protestants and Catholics as belonging to one group.

These nuances of supergroup preference are not readily distinguishable in large-scale statistical surveys of attitudes in Northern Ireland because of the subtlety and circumstantial nature of their operation. But large-scale surveys have shown that, to some extent, both Catholics and Protestants have unrealistic and inappropriate supergroup allegiances. The (Southern) Irish are less than ecstatic about the reality of a United Ireland (Cruise O'Brien, 1972; MacGreil, 1977) and the British are not overjoyed at the prospect of the continued membership of Northern Ireland in the United Kingdom.

This chapter has been concerned with relevant groups in Northern Ireland, the influences upon and between those groups and the attitudes held by group members. The evidence reviewed has suggested that 'the Northern Ireland problem', namely the inability of Catholics and Protestants to find a political compromise which would enable them to live amicably together is, in reality, two problems.

The problem for Protestants is that they have very strong objections to a number of aspects of Catholicism and those objections are underpinned by a complicated psychological network of fears and misapprehensions about the political power and dexterity of the Roman Catholic Church. These fears are reinforced as they look south of the border to a country where Catholicism dominates and divorce, and abortion are prohibited. Although the sale of contraceptives in certain circumstances has just been made legal in the Republic, the legislation remains more deferential to the Irish Catholic hierarchy than subservient to the actual needs of the community.

For Catholics, the problem is simpler. They merely dislike loyalist politics although from the most recent data available (O'Donnell, 1977), it seems that in approximately 1974, they disliked Protestants as people as a result of the conflict of recent years. However, because of the simpler, less deeply-seated nature of this outlook, one can anticipate that Catholic attitudes towards Protestants will be capable of significant improvement in the right circumstances.

CHAPTER THREE

People under Stress

In most parts of Northern Ireland, the physical encroachments of the troubles are relatively few and comprise such things as restrictions on parking in, and access to central areas of the town, occasional, often lethargic, searches of shopping bags on entering stores and other minor inconveniences which have long since merged into the quite unremarkable paraphernalia of normality in Ulster today. For the most part, even the suburbs of Belfast and Londonderry conform to this pattern although the central areas of these cities present a much sharper divergence from pre-trouble normality with military personnel and machinery much in evidence, more stringent and bothersome security measures together with the accumulated evidence of the focus of terrorist activity over the years in the form of gutted buildings, bomb-damage sales and reconstruction.

However, in some areas of Northern Ireland during the present conflict, this contemporary normality has not prevailed and the troubles have remained very close to the consciousness of the people who live in them. These are areas where much of the communal violence has taken place or which are so close to such areas that the threat of overspill or contagion has been present. Although the level of violence has dropped considerably in recent years, the fact that the conflict continues and that it could escalate once again, tends to maintain the pressure, even if at a somewhat lower level, on the people of these areas.

The studies examined here concern, inevitably, the most dramatic symptoms of stress of the communal violence and conflict. It is not the purpose of this chapter to dwell on the more tangible symptoms of the strife which have, in any case, been more than adequately depicted and tabulated in news media around the world. Nor is it the intention to offer some unfamiliar psychological terminology to describe the immediate feelings of those who have suffered the loss of friends and relatives or watched their communities being destroyed. Rather the aim is to examine the more enduring psychological consequences of these events.

Surprisingly, perhaps, adverse conditions do not necessarily produce adverse psychological reactions. Studies of the effects of war-time conditions on civilians in England in World War II yield the nearest equivalent in terms of the cultural norms of the people under study and in terms of prevalent psychiatric diagnostic practice. Such studies indicate that there was no general increase in psychiatric illness, (Massey, 1941; Lewis, 1942; Hopkins, 1943) although in provincial areas there was a slight rise in the incidence of short-lived neurotic reactions (Lewis, 1942). Even the severe London air-raids appeared to occasion relatively little well-defined neurotic illness (Atkin, 1941), although numerous acute emotional reactions did occur (Harris, 1941; Pegg, 1940). Many people with a previous history of neurotic illness seemed remarkably impervious to the stress of air-raids and some actually seemed to improve (Hemphill, 1941; Brown, 1941). In Coventry, which suffered some of the heaviest bombing in Britain during the war, there was a marked decrease in attendance at psychiatric out-patient clinics (Massey, 1941).

However, war-time Britain was a situation in which old rivalries and differences of opinion were buried in a united effort to resist the enemy without. In Ulster today, the situation is almost the complete reverse : old rivalries and differences have been dragged up from the past and given renewed life in a struggle which questions the very existence of the state and in which the enemy is within, and not even readily identifiable. In Britain there was an emergency coalition government : in Ulster, because of the inability of the political leaders to form a government acceptable to both communities, direct rule administration from Westminster has replaced the local parliament. On the other hand, the physical environments have some distinct similarities. Both lack some of the facilities of normal life. Both have the random and unpredictable possibility of bomb explosions, and the result of these explosions lies all around as a reminder of the state of war in which they live.

There is evidence of similar resistance to psychological illness

C

in civil war situations which more closely approximate the current situation in Northern Ireland, as for example in the American civil war (Hammond, 1883), the Franco-Prussian war (Legrande du Saulle, 1871) and the Spanish civil war (Mira, 1939). However, the difference in culture, time and psychiatric opinion and practice make these studies largely unacceptable as providing realistic comparable data.

Early newspaper reports after the severe Belfast troubles of summer 1969 claimed that there was a dramatic increase in the incidence of mental illness in the troubled areas, although the Secretary of Belfast's main mental hospital reported no significant increase in admission rates (Thompson, 1969). One GP was reported to have prescribed more than five times the usual number of tranquillisers. To clarify this discrepancy and more generally to look at the relationship between stress and the civil conflict, Fraser (1971b), a Belfast psychiatrist, analysed Belfast hospital admission and out-patient referral rates for psychiatric illness before and after the 1969 troubles, taking into account the degree of disturbance in the area of residence of the patients. In addition, he compared drug prescription rates before and after the 1969 troubles by GPs whose practices were in high, intermediate and low trouble areas. At the time of Fraser's study, the scale of the troubles in Belfast was such that only a small area of Belfast fell into the low trouble area classification as being entirely free from overt disturbance.

In terms of psychiatric illness, Fraser found that it was not in the areas of high civil disturbances that pre- and post-trouble differences occurred but rather in areas of intermediate disturbance, often adjacent to the worst trouble spots. Here, male out-patient referrals for psychoses rose from four in 1968 to nineteen in 1969, a difference which is statistically significant at the 0·01 level.*

In addition to differences in male psychoses (usually, but not

---

* This means that the chances are one hundred to one against such an increase occurring merely by chance, as part of the normal year to year fluctuations in such figures. More generally, such p-values, as they are known, reflect the confidence which we can have that a given difference or result is not due to chance factors. The smaller the p-value, the greater the confidence. Hence a result statistically significant at the 0·001 level (p<0·001) means that the chances are one thousand to one against such a result being due to chance factors, and so forth.

always, the most debilitating and severe mental disorders), Fraser also found that male out-patients referrals for neuroses rose from fourteen to twenty-six and female admissions to hospital for neuroses rose from fifty-six to seventy-eight in the areas of inter-mediate trouble. Both of these differences fell just outside the 0·05 level of statistical significance, the somewhat arbitrary con-ventional level of confidence as defined in footnote on p.54,* below which scientists prefer to suspend judgment in the validity of their findings Since, however, Fraser notes that the return of figures from hospitals is often delayed by several months and that an increase of one in either of the two 1969 figures in question would tip the differences into the realm of acceptable statistical significance, it would, perhaps, be unwise to ignore these results, particularly in the context of the small number of studies on which we can draw to form a picture of the psychological effects of the disturbances.

In the worst affected areas and the least affected area, there were no significant differences in terms of psychoses or neuroses for either men or women, although the numbers are so low for the least affected area that they preclude the possibility of mean-ingful assessment of differences.

The second part of Fraser's (1971b) study dealing with pre-scription rates of hypnotics, anti-depressants and tranquillisers by general practitioners in the three areas is much less satisfactory in terms of the validity of the data and, therefore, of the con-fidence which we can place on conclusions drawn from it. The author himself is obviously aware of this problem, since he calls into the question the degree to which the practices are exclusively serving the inhabitants of the areas of the city studied. There are further difficulties of interpretation caused by increases in the populations of the areas under study between 1968 and 1969 and by a general annual increase in the rate of tranquilliser prescriptions in Northern Ireland as a whole, apparently ante-cedent and unrelated to the troubles.

However, in a sub-study reported by Fraser (1971b) of two central practices in each of the three areas, which Fraser felt would be most likely to draw exclusively from the inhabitants of these areas, a statistically highly significant increase ($p < 0.001$) in the rate of prescription of tranquillisers was found between August and September 1968 in the worst riot areas, but not in the other areas. The increases ranged from 26 per cent to 135 per cent compared with increases from zero per cent to 25 per cent in the intermediate and peaceful areas.

A study published in the same year by another Belfast psychiatrist (Lyons, 1971a), looked at a number of characteristics of those who attended three general practices for psychiatric reasons within the riot areas of West Belfast during the period August 15 to September, 1969. This was undoubtedly the area of most severe disturbance examined by Fraser (1971), although he does not name the areas he studied. Lyons came to the somewhat suspect conclusion that of 217 such patients, the stress of the riots appeared to be a major contributory factor in the psychiatric condition of all of them, speculating that patients with unrelated psychiatric conditions did not attend their doctors during this period because of the difficulty and fear of travelling. It could be argued that only those least affected by the troubles would undertake the journey to their doctor's surgery and that those most affected would remain in the comparative safety of their own homes. In any case, fear of travelling to the doctor because of the troubles could hardly be symptomatic of psychiatric conditions unrelated to the troubles.

Bearing this difficulty in mind, Lyons found among the patients a preponderance of women (162 compared to 55 men), a high percentage of unemployed (31·8 per cent) and of lower socio-economic groups. The latter point is not so much a finding of any theoretical significance as an indication that Lyons' sample was true in at least one respect to the population from which it was derived, since West Belfast is an area of low socio-economic status. In regard to the high percentage of unemployed (even for this area of Belfast), it is true, as Lyons notes, that there is some evidence that the unemployed are more prone to psychiatric complaints (Hinkle and Wolff, 1958) but Lyons' study does not illuminate which, if either, is the hen and which the egg. That is to say we have no way of knowing whether the unemployment is a contributory factor to the psychiatric disorder or vice-versa, or whether both the unemployment and the psychiatric illness are caused by some other factor.

The most common diagnosis was acute situational state (ninety-three patients), a strong but short-lived emotional experience. Just over 50 per cent of these patients had no previous record of psychiatric symptoms indicating that this reaction to the troubles, or a milder form of it, could be reasonably common in the communities most seriously affected, especially among women who comprised seventy-four of the ninety-three so diagnosed.

The next most common diagnosis (fifty-six patients) was of anxiety state, a rather more prolonged disturbance (classified by Lyons as lasting more than one week), followed by reactive depression (thirty-two patients), hysterical reaction (twelve patients) and phobic reaction (nine patients). An assortment of psychological and psychosomatic disturbances made up the remaining diagnoses. Apart from those diagnosed as acute situational state, a more or less normal anxiety in the particularly intense stress of the time and place, the majority of patients in other categories had had previous psychiatric treatment. The high incidence of short-lived emotional reactions is consistent with the weight of evidence from British war-time studies mentioned previously. The fact that so many of the patients had previously been treated for psychiatric disorders indicates that, in general, it is the vulnerable who show the first effects of the stress, as Lyons (1973a, 1973b) notes in a subsequent study.

The most common symptom, reported by 187 patients, was affective disturbance, or emotional upset, most commonly general fear but also in some cases specific fears, for example, of loud noise, of attack and of going out. Insomnia, anxiety, loss of appetite, phobias, general nervousness and depression, in that order of frequency, were commonly reported symptoms in the sample of patients.

Lyons (1972a), in a study of the incidence of depression in Belfast and County Down, the most peaceful of the six counties of Northern Ireland, found that, compared to the average for the years 1963-68, there was a reduction in the recorded incidence of depression in all areas of Belfast for both men and women during the period 1 September 1969 to 31 August 1970. This contrasted with an increase in the incidence of depression for males only in County Down.

Looking more closely at his data in terms of the incidence of depression in particular areas of Belfast, Lyons (1972a) reaches some conclusions which his data does not justify. For example, he describes the reduction in the incidence of depression in West Belfast as 'much more significant than that of South Belfast'

(p. 343). In fact, what the data shows is that the reduction in West Belfast is statistically significant at the 0·01 level whereas the reduction in South Belfast is statistically significant at the 0.05 level. As explained on p.54, these figures relate to the confidence which one can have that the reductions are 'real' and not just due to chance fluctuations in the incidence of depression in either case. Hence, the West Belfast reduction is somewhat more reliable as an indicator of real change than is the South Belfast reduction on the basis of the figures which Lyons analysed in his study. However, one cannot infer, as Lyons does on the basis of these figures, that the reduction in West Belfast was 'more significant' than the reduction in South Belfast. As a matter of fact, the reduction in South Belfast, calculating on Lyons' own figures, was comparatively larger than the reduction in West Belfast, 21 per cent compared to 16 per cent.

Nonetheless, however the figures are computed, there was general decrease in recorded depression rates during 1969-70 in Belfast, compared to an increase for males only in County Down, a relatively peaceful county. Lyons tries to relate this data to the psychoanalytic theory of depression (Abraham, 1911; Freud, 1917) which basically claims that depressive illness is caused by the inhibition of aggressive impulses and responses to frustration. Thus, in Western society where overt aggression is normally disapproved and suppressed, depression is endemic (Storr, 1968), or so the theory goes. Belfast in 1969-71 would constitute an exception to the general rule of the suppression of aggressive impulses and, therefore, provides a partial test of the theory.

It is true that reports on psychiatric casualties among combat troops in Vietnam show a low incidence of depressive illness (Duy San, 1969; Tischler, 1969) and in so far as the residents of Belfast in the particular period of 1969-70 can be thought of as being in and around a conflict situation, Lyons (1972a) data is concordant with the general thrust of the theory. However, the effect could be due to some other cause than the release of aggression.

Although there is a rather gross alignment of fact and theory, a closer analysis of the data reveals that the relationship cannot be sustained without the addition of some major and precarious assumptions. For example, the incidence of depressive illness among males in an area of severe rioting, inner West Belfast, shows a similar reduction since the start of the troubles to that of one of the most peaceful areas of the city, outer South Belfast. In inner West Belfast the incidence drops from an average of forty-seven during 1964-68 to thirty-eight during 1969-70 while in outer South Belfast the decrease is from an average of forty-six during 1964-68 to thirty-seven during 1969-70.

We must assume that since there was little physical evidence of outward-directed aggression in outer South Belfast, the aggression took some other form, for example angry thoughts and conversation. And if it is reasonable to assume that, then it is also reasonable to assume that the males of County Down (whose boundary begins at outer South Belfast) would have felt and expressed anger in much the same way and for much the same reasons, but the incidence of male depressive illness in County Down increased during the period rather than decreased.

There are several other aspects of the data which are equally embarrassing for the theory and it is, therefore, difficult to accept a psychoanalytic interpretation of them. Certainly, Lyons' explanation of the County Down figures appears incongruous and speculative, even if one does accept his theoretical base. He notes that the men 'may feel more frustration at being unable to participate actively in aggression but who see [sic] reports of violence daily through the local news media' (p. 344).

Again, this study highlights the preponderance of women among those who succumb to mental illness, the ratio being two or three to one in Belfast and just under two to one in County Down.

Four studies have looked at the incidence of suicide in Northern Ireland in recent years, namely Lyons (1972a, 1973a) and O'Malley (1972, 1975). Lyons' (1972a) study looks at the official figures for suicide from 1964 to 1970 as supplied by the Registrar General and compares them with the equivalent figures for homicide. His 1973 (a) study extends the figures to September, 1972.

Lyons' thesis is again psychoanalytic and based on the 'hydraulic' theory of psychic energy, so dubbed because it proposes that the energies which propel our behaviour have a natural level, just as liquid in a U-tube will find a level in which the height of the liquid in both arms of the U is identical. If for any reason the pressure in one arm varies so that the level of the liquid alters in that arm, there will be a corresponding change in the level of liquid in the other arm. Thus, in relation to the suicide/homicide data, the theory runs that our natural levels of aggression will be directed outwards against others (hence homicide) or they will be directed inwards against ourselves (hence suicide). In normal times in Western society, there will be a pressure on the expression of aggression towards others so that levels of suicide will be higher. Conversely in times of conflict where violence towards others may be condoned or encouraged, the suicide rate should drop.

Certainly, phenomena do occasionally occur which can be interpreted in this theory's favour. For example, every country involved in the Second World War showed a decrease in suicide rates. But the reality is much more complex than that. Suicide is more frequent among whites than non-whites (in the United States), among older persons than younger, in higher socio-economic levels than lower and among persons with a high rather than a low I.Q. Homicide, on the other hand, is more often committed by non-Whites (in the United States), by younger people, those low in socio-economic level and by those low in I.Q. (Rosen and Gregory, 1975). To some extent, the cultural norms on the acceptability of overt aggression affect these typical findings on homicide perpetrators. But nonetheless, homicide and suicide are typically committed by different types of people, whereas the hydraulic theory is only really put to the test when the same people are subjected to different circumstances.

Far from having an inverse or hydraulic relationship, suicide and homicide figures from the United States show a positive relationship. For example, the correlation* between suicide and homicide from 1960 to 1969 (using US Dept. of Health, Educa-

---

* Correlation measures the degree to which two sets of variables are linearly related to each other in a positive or negative direction. In a positive correlation between two variables, as one rises, the other tends also to rise and as one falls, the other tends also to fall. For example, there is a positive correlation between age and facial wrinkles—the older we are, the more facial wrinkles we have. In a negative correlation, as one variable rises the other tends to fall and vice-versa. For example, there is a negative correlation between age and running speed—the older we are, the lower the running speed which we can achieve. The correlation coefficient measures the strength of these tendencies and is expressed numerically as varying between -1 (perfect negative correlation) to $+1$ (perfect positive correlation). In practice, psychological phenomena are never perfectly correlated,

tion and Welfare statistics) in the United States is +0·43 indicating that they tend to some degree to rise and fall together rather than to rise and fall in contrast to each other. The correlation between homicide and suicide in the figures presented by Lyons (1973a) is – 0·27 which is an inverse or hydraulic relationship, if a somewhat weak one. The point is that there is no general or consistent inverse relationship between homicide and suicide.

The simplest explanation of the decreasing suicide rates is as a consequence of the decreasing depression rates. Suicide is a natural by-product of depression. The estimates vary from study to study but findings by Rennie (1942) and Lundquist (1945) suggest that the risk of suicide in a patient hospitalised at some time in his life for depression is about five hundred times the United States national average. Pokorny's (1964) data puts the figures at a less hair-raising twenty-five times the expected rate and Temoche, Pugh and MacMahon (1964) computed a ratio of thirty-six times the average. Whatever the exact figure, we may reasonably expect to find any decrease in depression rates reflected in a decrease in suicide rates.

O'Malley (1972, 1975) has looked at suicide and attempted suicide between 1967 and 1973 in Northern Ireland and found that the decrease in completed suicide is accompanied by a very large increase in attempted suicide as indicated by a 300 per cent increase in attempted suicide admissions to the Mater Hospital in Belfast. Although the attempted suicide rates have been increasing elsewhere in the British Isles (for example there was a 221 per cent increase in such admissions to the Newcastle-upon-Tyne General Hospital in the North of England over the period 1960-1969), the Mater admission rates are very high.

O'Malley (1975) studied one hundred consecutive attempted suicide admissions in 1972 in some detail, which gives us some indication of the likely characteristics of attempted suicide patients in general in Northern Ireland. Once again, women are the predominant sufferers, in the ratio of approximately two to one. The Mater patients appear roughly to reflect the Northern Irish religious denomination ratios, 41 per cent Catholic and 59 per cent other (mainly Church of Ireland and Presbyterian). In terms of the Belfast population, which is 27·5 per cent Catholic, the proportion of Catholics is high. This could simply be because the Mater is a Catholic hospital, administered by the church, al-

c*

though having no intentional denominational bias in terms of patients. Although the Mater is held in very high regard as a hospital by both communities in Belfast and is a teaching hospital associated with Queen's University Faculty of Medicine, it probably does have a higher percentage of Catholic patients than other Belfast hospitals.

Married female attempted suicide patients were almost twice as numerous as single females, but the ratio was similar for men. As far as age spread is concerned, the twenty to twenty-nine age group was largest at 37 per cent, but there were also considerable numbers in other age groups : 24 per cent in the ten to nineteen age group, 16 per cent in the thirty to thirty-nine group and 14 per cent in the forty to forty-nine group.

In terms of the sex ratios and age spread, these attempted suicide statistics contrast with completed suicide statistics generally, in which men are most numerous and tend to have an increasing suicide rate with age while women reach a peak at forty-five to sixty-five, declining thereafter.

O'Malley (1975) also sets this data in the context of psychoanalytic theory, but the effort is misdirected. In terms of psychoanalytic theory, there is no *a priori* reason to differentiate suicide and attempted suicide. Both are examples of aggression directed inwards against the self and, therefore, both should decrease in times of strife when the normal inhibitions on outward-directed aggression are removed.

As one would expect from the relationship between depression and suicide noted above, depressive illness was a prominent feature of the attempted suicide sample, depressive states being diagnosed in 44 per cent of the cases. But only 2 per cent of the attempted suicide sample were diagnosed as endogenously depressive (the depression arising from within the individual rather than as a reaction to outside events) compared to 23 per cent suffering from reactive depression, giving a reactive/endogenous ratio of 23 : 2 or 11·5 : 1 in the group. Lyons' (1972a) data for the reported incidence of depression in Northern Ireland between 1964 and 1970, however, shows a much more equal reactive/endogenous ratio of approximately 12 : 10 or 1·2 : 1, which means that the attempted suicide depressives are quite distinct from depressives in general in Northern Ireland.

Perhaps the most striking point about the sample of attempted suicide patients studied by O'Malley (1975) is that 40 per cent were classified as suffering from personality disorder, a somewhat nebulous and indistinct 'rag bag' category of individuals with various difficulties, such as immaturity and inadequacy, who would fall at the vulnerable end of the normal spectrum. It is also pertinent to note the low incidence of psychoses among the attempted suicide sample compared to a comparison group of patients, admitted at the same time, who had no suicidal background, in other words, the more usual psychiatric patient. Psychoses were present in 23 per cent of the comparison group compared to only 10 per cent of the attempted suicide group indicating for O'Malley (1975) that '. . . the rise in attempted suicide is not related to serious mental illness.' (p. 108).

Putting all these factors together, it seems quite clear that attempted suicide patients in Northern Ireland cannot simply be classified as inept suicide victims, but rather as a quite distinct and separate group. Almost 50 per cent of the attempted suicide patients were either 'definitely' or 'probably' driven to their action by some aspect of the communal violence, in contrast to only 18 per cent of the comparison group whose illness was either 'definitely' or 'probably' precipitated by the troubles. The indications are that attempted suicide is a reaction of the vulnerable fringe of society in Northern Ireland's troubled areas, either of those whose problems would fall within the normal range of psychological difficulties, such as immaturity, or those whose mental disorder is not sufficiently severe to prevent an acceptable level of functioning in their home environments.

On the latter point, it should be noted that the diagnoses of the attempted suicide patients were made after and in the context of their attempted suicidal behaviour. Unfortunately, O'Malley does not appear to have looked at the previous history of mental illness in these patients. It seems probable, however, that many would have had no previous history of classifiable mental illness and that without such a dramatic 'symptom', their clinical condition may never have come to light. In that sense, therefore, it is possible to view attempted suicide as a dramatic, infrequent but nonetheless real indication of the prolonged impact of bloodshed and violence on those sections of the community most affected by the troubles.

It is possible to take a contrary point of view and argue that

since such people are 'only' that small, most vulnerable section
of the community, it is inappropriate to take their behaviour as
indicative of a more general effect on the population within the
worst affected areas. This line of argument, however, reaches
its logical conclusion at the point where the 'real' population is
defined by the fact that it shows little or no reaction to the events
around it, which is patently absurd.

The suggestion here is that the dramatic increase in the incidence of attempted suicide is indicative of the degree to which
the stress of living in violence-prone communities in Northern
Ireland is capable of driving the individual in the extreme case.
The more normal, psychologically sturdier members of the communities involved may be able to avoid perceiving the same
degree of stress and/or may cope with it in a more productive
manner but the increasing attempted suicide rates indicate, in
some small degree at least, that this is not necessarily an everlasting immunity. Vulnerability is a relative concept; there are
not simply the vulnerable and the invulnerable in life. Today's
invulnerable may be tomorrow's victims.

We have looked at those who by dint of their personal characteristics have suffered most from the trouble within their community. However, a study by Lyons (1974b) reports on those
whose experience has been particularly harrowing, namely the
victims of bomb explosions.

To some extent, Lyons (1974b) sample of one hundred such
patients were self-selected since they actively sought medical
help. Those with severe physical injuries are under-represented
as they are treated in general hospitals. There were fifty-two
males and forty-eight females in the study, which probably under-
represents males, since factories and bars frequented by men
have been favoured bomb targets. There were, inevitably, rather
more patients in the lower socio-economic groups than is the
case in the Belfast population generally, since poorer, working
class districts of the city have borne the brunt of bombing.

Most patients had several symptoms and some sort of affective
or emotional disturbance was present in over 90 per cent, the
most common being anxiety or anxiety coupled with some sort
of phobia. The phobias noted were agoraphobia (fear of open
spaces)—36 per cent; separation phobia (fear of being parted
from loved ones)—12 per cent; car phobia (fear of parked

cars)—6 per cent; and crowd phobia (fear of crowds)—3 per cent. As Lyons notes, all of these phobias are adaptive in the sense that the patients were seeking to avoid potentially dangerous situations within their environment. Sixty-three per cent were suffering from insomnia, 37 per cent from irritability (leading to marital discord in some cases), 24 per cent from nightmares and 22 per cent from depression, mainly reactive depression although the depth of depression in two cases was such that electro-convulsive therapy (ECT) was required.

Rating the degree of disturbance on clinical grounds, Lyons found that 62 per cent were slightly disturbed, 33 per cent moderately disturbed and only 5 per cent severely disturbed. There was a statistically significant ($p < 0.002$) relationship between age and severity of illness with most younger patients showing only minor disturbance.

In general, the rate of improvement in the patients was fairly good, 46 per cent making a rapid recovery, 37 per cent moderate recovery and 16 per cent making a slow recovery. Younger patients recovered more quickly. Lyons notes that the natural history of the condition appeared to be one of fairly rapid improvement over a period of six months to one year following the explosion.

Lyons also obtained some details of the circumstances of the explosions in which the patients were involved, for example what the patient was doing at the time and how far he or she was from the explosion. No significant correlations were found between any such variable and the severity of illness. There was no significant relationship found between severity of illness and physical injury suffered as a result of the explosion (although, as mentioned above, there were no serious injuries among the patients) nor was there a significant relationship with whether others had been killed or severely injured in the explosion. Lyons aptly comments that 'The fairly rapid rate of recovery seen in the Belfast patients is surprising as one would think the patients' symptoms would be constantly reinforced by the continued bombing campaign in the city, but it would appear that a remarkable resilience and tolerance of this type of stress can develop.' (p. 19)

Apart from the methodological problems of some of the above studies and the fact that a relatively restricted range of psychological phenomena has been studied, most of the data, which they have presented, relates to Belfast. This creates a problem in trying to synthesise them into an impression of the effects of the conflict on people in troubled areas of Northern Ireland generally. It is not possible to state with any authority the degree to which the conclusions reached would generalise to other troubled areas. In so far as Belfast has perhaps suffered the worst of the violence, it may be that the toll there has been to some extent higher. However, it would seem unlikely that the nature of the effects would be substantially different elsewhere especially in areas, such as Londonderry, which have also suffered much. In any case, Belfast contains approximately one-third of the population of Northern Ireland and, therefore, data on the Belfast population must weigh heavily in any general assessment of the province.

In summary, then, several points have emerged. First, while men have suffered the brunt of the physical damage, it appears that more women have suffered from psychological disturbance as a result of the communal upheaval, as evidenced by referral and admission rates for psychiatric disturbance in Belfast and in Northern Ireland generally. However, there may be an element of distortion in this picture because typically, while there are no sex differences in the prevalence of total psychological abnormality generally, women have a greater tendency to develop depression and other neurotic disorders while men show a consistently higher incidence of anti-social disturbance (Dohrenwend and Dohrenwend, 1967). These differences may be due to cultural stereotypes of what constitutes appropriate behaviour for men and women. It is expected and acceptable for women to display emotion and for men to display aggression.

Lyons (1975) comments that since the troubles began 'one has seldom seen a psychopath referred to the ordinary out-patient clinic' (p. 293). While one could not regard such a remark as evidence, the notion that individuals, who would previously have been under treatment for some form of anti-social disturbance, are now pillars of their local community has some currency in casual conversation in Northern Ireland. In all probability there is an element of truth in this idea and it is likely that a few individuals, mainly males, have found a context in which their anti-social tendencies can be channelled into acceptable forms of expression in their local communities. However the incidence is probably lower than the non-sympathetic might hope. This topic will be more thoroughly examined in the following chapter.

The sex difference in the psychological effects of the troubles is much more readily explained in terms of the prevalence of male opportunity for socialisation in groups in the troubled areas which provides purpose, company and support for men whether at work, in paramilitary organisations, in community organisations or in the local pub. Despite the turmoil, women still have all the usual domestic responsibilities and consequent isolation. Fraser's (1971b) finding that areas of intermediate disturbance are most affected in terms of psychiatric disturbance is consistent with this interpretation since the stress is present in these areas but the same degree of community organisation and involvement is not.

The community stress has had a curious effect in that it appears that there is a further differential influence in operation. The decrease in depression and suicide rates seems to indicate that for some, the troubles have brought purpose to a previously empty or difficult existence. Colloquially, such people could be said to have found something else to get involved in rather than themselves.

On the other hand, the increase in attempted suicide tends to suggest that a different section of the population finds the stress difficult to bear. An educated guess would be that such people are those who are not heavily involved in their community goals, either personally or ideologically.

It is probable that there is an inestimable but possibly substantial middle ground of people who manage to get on with their lives apparently relatively unaffected by the entire catastrophe which surrounds them. The resilience of the bomb victims studied by Lyons (1974b) supports this hypothesis although it is possible that this middle ground is partially held by increased prescription rates of sedatives by GPs in troubled areas, as noted by Fraser (1971b).

Adaptation to stress is characteristic of all animals including man (Dubos, 1965) and in lower animals may be substantially and parsimoniously explained in neurophysiological terms (Thompson and Spencer, 1966). The evidence reviewed in this chapter, therefore, represents a re-affirmation of human adaptability to adverse environmental conditions. Life goes on in

Northern Ireland, but the mode of adaptation is undoubtedly more complex in humans and the specific pattern of adaptation will reflect both the personality of the individual concerned and, particularly, his cognitive perspective of the situation (Lazarus, 1966). Effectively, this means that there will be a wide variety of coping patterns but all will share one common general feature, namely that objectively stressful events in the environment will have less and less subjective psychological impact. This is the essence of the definition of adaptation chosen by Glass and Singer (1972) in their analysis of urban stress.

In effect, it is often difficult to discern, even in the individual case, what the underlying dimensions of the coping behaviour are. For instance, is the person who says 'To hell with it, the sooner they all shoot each other, the better' characteristically insensitive or has he formulated a perspective in relation to the troubles which puts him at a comfortable psychological distance from them? Even that is a naïve question since personality characteristics undoubtedly will affect the range of cognitive perspectives which are open to the individual.

However, there is a body of opinion that this very adaptation or coping may entail a cumulative psychological cost (Selye, 1956; Bastowitz et al., 1955; Dubos, 1965; Wohlwill, 1966, 1970). This cost would perhaps only become evident after the environmental stresses have ceased either because the act of coping delays or masks the actual toll of the stress so that it does not become evident until coping is no longer necessary, or because constant vigilance and coping is itself stressful if forced to become an endless process. Hence when the stress terminates, a double reaction occurs, not only to the stressful environmental circumstances, but also to the strain of coping (Glass and Singer, 1972).

The terms 'cognitive overload' or 'informational overload' are sometimes used to describe such situations where the stress of the environment is so severe that people adapt to their surroundings by shutting out all but the most necessary information. They develop adaptive styles which reduce the overload to acceptable levels, but it appears that the process is often an overreaction so that important information is also excluded from consideration, or important events do not elicit the response which they justify. To some extent the baby is thrown out with the bath water. Milgram (1970) has examined this process in large American cities, noting that less and less time is devoted to each stimulus input, with the result that social responsibility is reduced, everyday civilities are relatively absent and there is little willingness to assist strangers.

Perhaps the best known incident which illustrates something of what Milgram has in mind is that of Kitty Genovese who lived in the Queens area of New York city. Returning home from work on the 13 March 1964 at 3.30 a.m., she parked her car in the parking lot and walked towards her apartment. As she did so, a man attacked and stabbed her. She screamed, the man ran off, but moments later returned and stabbed her again. Lights went on in many apartments and the attacker got in his car and drove off. However, a couple of minutes later, he returned, by which time Miss Genovese had crawled to the back of her apartment building, and stabbed her once again, this time fatally.

Eventually, at 3.50 a.m., a neighbour called the police, but not before phoning a friend for advice and then going to the apartment of an elderly woman to ask her to make the call. Thirty-eight people in all silently witnessed this horrible sequence of events. Apparently they did not want to get involved. The case aroused much public comment and academic interest and a film was made, loosely based on selected facts of the case (for example, the assailant, who was in fact a Negro, is portrayed as white in the film). In 1974 another woman was killed in the same place. Again people heard her scream and again ignored it.

The citizens of New York have adjusted to the violence and suffering in their environment by ignoring most of it. It would not be possible to survive psychologically in New York if one were to dwell on the human implications of each of the murders that are committed in that city (1,640 in 1975, according to the *New York Times* Index, 1976). Even calculating murder rates per 100,000 population, the murder rate in Northern Ireland is small by comparison to that of New York, and minute in comparison to some other United States cities such as Atlanta, Houston, Cleveland and Detroit (the New York murder rate, because of the geographical spread and huge population of the city, masks an astronomical murder rate in the downtown areas such as Manhattan).

These circumstances have obtained for decades in New York

and presumably will continue for decades to come. New Yorkers grow up with it and have a lifetime to adjust to it. The stress in Northern Ireland arose somewhat suddenly and, it is to be hoped, will disappear in the foreseeable future. But even in the relatively short period of its existence, similar phenomena to the Kitty Genovese case have occurred in Northern Ireland. For example, in February 1973, a group of young men tied a screaming woman to a lamppost in a Protestant area of West Belfast and savagely beat her while residents watched silently from their windows. The woman was reportedly left hanging for more than one hour in bitter weather without anyone coming to her aid, despite her loud screams. When the police investigated the matter, no one on the street admitted to hearing anything, although people living three streets away said they did.

Such behaviour is uncharacteristic of the Northern Irish, who usually go out of their way to be friendly and helpful to others. Even in Belfast, a city of half a million inhabitants, the manners and ambience of the people have been rather more rural than urban (Spencer, 1974). Consistent with these impressions is the fact that the crime rates in Northern Ireland have, prior to the present troubles, tended to be very low in comparison to other regions of the United Kingdom for example (see Chapter Six).

How do people come to behave in the manner which the above incidents so vividly describe and, more generally and less dramatically, how do people avoid the heavy psychological burden of the events that surround them?

Some people, in Northern Ireland, to my knowledge, reduce the environmental input simply by not watching local news (which often dwells on local violence) and by skipping reports of trouble in their reading of local newspapers. If they do watch TV news at all, they tend to watch national news, that is British or Irish news (in the areas where Southern Irish television can be received). Hence they only hear about developments in Ulster important enough or sensational enough to be reported nationally and find more than enough to worry about in reports of the latest price inflation, the British government's newest wage restriction or the next major strike.

Those who do watch the local news sometimes, do so to see what is happening 'out there' and so are able to sustain the belief that the events depicted do not and will not affect their lives.

Such an adaptive cognitive adjustment is usually effective in distancing oneself from the troubles, which are usually very localised, but events such as the fall of the Stormont government and the Protestant general strike of 1974 severely dented that particular armour, at least temporarily.

However, such an adaptation has not been possible for those who have been in the midst of it, such as those who silently witnessed the callous beating of a woman from behind their curtains in West Belfast. But other mechanisms are available.

Lerner (1965) has proposed that people believe that they get what they deserve and conversely that they deserve what they get. When they see suffering or misfortune, they tend to believe that the unfortunate victim merited his or her fate. The gist of his argument is that this is a necessary mechanism for the sake of peace of mind, the unpalatable alternative being a world governed by chance, in which the next victim may be oneself.

Lerner and Simmons (1966) carried out an experiment to test this hypothesis in which female college students observed another female student (in fact, an accomplice of the experimenters) receive severe and painful shocks for making errors in a learning task. The subjects, who were led to believe that they would continue to see the victim suffer in a subsequent session (and hence that this was not a single, isolated event in the victim's life) gave low evaluations of the victim's characteristics when subsequently required to rate them. Rejection and devaluation also occurred when the subjects knew they were relatively powerless to help the victim and was particularly strong when the victim was seen as a 'martyr' who was suffering for the sake of the subjects. In somewhat similar circumstances, Elms (1972) also found this tendency among subjects to derogate the characteristics of someone whom they had been ordered to shock (again, an accomplice of the experimenter).

There is always a danger in psychology of making broad generalisations from limited experimental evidence just because the evidence is experimental, and that danger is nowhere greater than in social psychology. Experiments in social psychology are, at best, good imitations of one of life's infinite facets and, in fact, there is not much experimental evidence to back up Lerner's hypothesis. Yet in certain important respects it conforms with one's general experience.

We do tend to think that the unemployed and those receiving welfare benefits are not trying hard enough, that people in ghettoes do not want to raise their standard of living and that unmarried mothers have only themselves to blame, even though these ideas would not bear much objective scrutiny (Ryan, 1976). Most of us would sooner take a stray cat into our lives than a stray child. In Britain, the Royal Society for the Prevention of Cruelty to Animals regularly receives more in charitable donations than the Royal Society for the Prevention of Cruelty to Children. I would guess that there is a tendency to imagine that one can help in the former case whereas in the latter, one can only scratch the surface. This contrasts with our usually sympathetic attitudes to accident and disaster victims (as long as the disasters do not occur too frequently in the same place or the victims do not need prolonged help).

So observers impute blame onto victims especially if they find themselves unable to help as is often the case in Ulster's most troubled communities where people may fear that their intervention on behalf of a victim would occasion violence against themselves, their homes or their families. Obviously, though this phenomenon is more pertinent to such communities, from what has been said above, people elsewhere in Northern Ireland should be prone to this reaction and indeed, in my experience, it was commonly remarked in the early years of the troubles amongst those not directly involved that anyone shot or injured 'must have been involved in something, just the same', lacing sympathy with imputed blame. My impression is that this reaction is diminishing a little in frequency as the evidence of innocent slaughter on all sides has accumulated.

In addition, it appears that in situations where help is required, it may be that the more people there are present, the less likely any one person will be to provide assistance. This could occur because the responsibility for action is diluted and because the very fact of no one helping may alter the perception of those involved so that they re-interpret the situation as not being an emergency (Darley and Latané, 1968; Latané and Darley, 1968). However, most of the research on helping behaviour happens to have been done with female subjects and it is possible that group size in potential helping situations may be more important with women (Lerner, Solomon and Brody, 1971; Schwartz and

Clausen, 1970). All the studies suggest women tend to help less often than men in emergencies, presumably largely as a result of socialisation which cast women in the role of helped and helpless, while casting men as gallant helpers (Severy, Brigham and Schlenker, 1976).

In conclusion, therefore, the adults of Northern Ireland's troubled areas have adapted with characteristic human resilience in the face of adversity. However, there are two reasons why the stress of conflict has had a superficially muted effect as indicated by the evidence reviewed in this chapter.

First, there has been a differential effect, on men as opposed to women and on some psychologically vulnerable groups as opposed to others. A common-sense expectation might have been that all the effects would be negative whereas it appears that some effects are, temporarily at least, positive while others are negative.

Second, the very process of coping with and adapting to the stress of communal violence and turmoil may have a latent effect which will not become apparent until the burden of coping is lifted. The cognitive defence mechanisms described above which shield people from the worst psychological strains of their environment will not disappear instantly on the cessation of violence, and indeed, may contribute to its prolongation. As noted previously, these reactions (or more correctly, the levels at which they are being adopted) are inappropriate to life in the province of Ulster in normal times. People may have to re-learn appropriate responses to others.

Equally, the coping process may be masking an inestimable strain as well as providing a stress of its own just as the legendary, grief-stricken performer insists that 'the show must go on'. The question that remains is what will be the eventual effect on these people and their community when the show is over.

CHAPTER FOUR

Terrorism

Terrorism is in the eye of the beholder. This point has been made, in one form or another, by several commentators on the phenomenon of international terrorism today (e.g. Friedlander, 1978). The topic of terrorism is so emotionally charged that it might be useful to expand a little on this point to facilitate a rational perusal of terrorism in Ireland.

A necessary defining condition of terrorism is that it involves atrocious behaviour and a lack of normal regard for human life and property in the pursuit of some objective. Thus, the bombing of Birmingham public houses in November 1974 by the Provisional IRA, in which twenty-one people were killed and 162 injured, was clearly an act of terrorism and universally condemned as such.

However, atrocious behaviour is not a sufficient condition of terrorism. One does not regard the British bombings of Dresden, the American bombing of Hiroshima or the German bombings of London as acts of terrorism. Yet these actions resulted in the death and mutilation of vast numbers of innocent civilians and the behaviour of the perpetrators was, numerically at least, more atrocious than the Birmingham pub bombings, and its effects more calculated and cold-blooded. A telephone warning, albeit far too late, was given of the Birmingham bombings and at least one of the perpetrators, filled with horror and regret at the consequences of his actions broke down under interrogation and made a full confession (Clutterbuck, 1978). No such redeeming features attend the other actions mentioned above.

What differences between these situations cause them to be perceived differently? Obviously, in the Dresden, Hiroshima and London bombings, the victims were inhabitants of a country with whom the perpetrators were at war and who might legitimately, if regrettably, expect to suffer the consequences of that fact. However, the Provisional IRA sees itself as at war with Britain and has frequently made that view explicit, although even its most fanatical members have expressed a lack of hostility towards the British public (e.g. MacStiofain, 1975).

It could be argued that the so-called 'war' being waged by the Provisional IRA is a one-sided affair, unlike World War II, with Britain as innocent victim, but the presence and activities of the British Army in Northern Ireland render that line of argument difficult to sustain. It is tempting to consider the possibility that in the intervening years since World War II, the Western world has become much more conscious of the humanitarian evils of conflict, albeit simultaneously devising ever more potent means for perpetrating such evil. However, recent American activities in Vietnam give the lie to that argument. Bowyer Bell's (1977) comment that 'Terrorists have neither the capacity nor the desire to kill great masses; only rulers have had both' (p. 41) is a valid current, as well as historical, reflection. In the Irish conflict, no-warning bombs in public places are the exception rather than the rule and terrorist organisations have agreed code-words with those to whom warnings are given in order to foil the would-be hoaxer.

In fact, it is extraordinarily difficult to provide a definition of terrorism which makes a rational psychological distinction between what terrorists do and what governments engaged in conflict actually do. Consider the following effort by Mickolus (1978) to define the focus of his study of transnational terrorism :

'The use, or threat of use, of anxiety-inducing extranormal violence for political purposes by an individual or group, whether acting for or in opposition to established governmental authority, when such action is intended to influence the attitudes and behaviour of a target group wider than the immediate victims and when, through the nationality or the foreign ties of its perpetrators, its location, the nature of its institutional or human victims, or the mechanics of its resolution its ramifications transcend national boundaries.' (p. 44)

Such a definition applies equally well to Dresden, Hiroshima, London, Vietnam and Birmingham.

But yet we do tend to perceive a difference between the Birmingham bombings and these other activities. We distinguish between the atrocious behaviour of soldiers in Northern Ireland (the best documented and clearest example of which occurred on 'Bloody Sunday' in Londonderry when thirteen civilians were shot dead) and the atrocious behaviour of Protestant and Catholic terrorists in Northern Ireland. Clearly the institutional mantle of some atrocious behaviour sets it in a different conceptual category.

However, even this distinction is not sufficient to pinpoint the basis of the general revulsion of terrorist activities in Northern Ireland for, as Clutterbuck (1975) has pointed out, we glamourise, to this day, the activities of the French Resistance, who were brutally cruel to their victims, whom they killed by stealth. Equally, it is difficult to counter the Provisionals' argument that the British government's attitude to terrorism is hypocritical in view of that government's tacit support for the Patriotic Front in Rhodesia (*Sunday Times*, 25 June 1978). It is, in fact, difficult to escape Clutterbuck's argument that the distinction ultimately boils down to a question of 'good guys' and 'bad guys' given the inescapable conclusion that atrocious behaviour is the norm in conflict situations, whoever it involves. The Americans could not avoid the inevitable descent to atavistic aggression in Vietnam (most dramatically exemplified in the My Lai case) nor have the forces of the British government been able to avoid the inevitable in Northern Ireland.

This descent to atrocious behaviour and its now customary subsequent public exposure, leads to the typical argument on behalf of the establishment that such tactics are necessary in dealing with the sort of tactics of the IRA/Vietcong/Nazis/Japanese, etc. In defence of the interrogation methods of the Royal Ulster Constabulary at Castlereagh Barracks, Utley used precisely this argument in the *Sunday Telegraph* recently (18 March 1979).

The problem with this line of argument is that it can invariably be used with equal validity by those to whom it is being applied. Thus the IRA would argue, and have argued, that their campaign is in response to the brutality visited upon their members and the Catholic population generally by the security forces in either acting directly against them or, in some cases, refusing to intervene on their behalf to protect them from Protestant sectarian attack. In so far as it is extremely rare in the affairs of men for the aetiology of a conflict to be fully and undeniably placed at the feet of one of the conflicting parties (and this is certainly not the case in Northern Ireland), then this particular argument suffers from perpetual rebound characteristics. Furthermore, it leads to the inevitable conclusion that one's standards of behaviour are directed by the actions of others and will deteriorate in response to any deterioration in those actions. This is, of course, perfectly true. While a terrorist organisation would have no problem in admitting this, or even proclaiming it, governments, especially those with virginal pretensions such as the British government, find it politically and diplomatically embarrassing to do so.

It is a popularly held opinion that terrorists are people who are evil men at worst, sick at best and frequently psychopathic. Thus, terrorist causes afford them some sort of semi-legitimate outlet for their anti-social tendencies which would, in normal circumstances, result in their running foul of the law. Another theme of popular discourse is that terrorist groups are composed of general ne'er-do-wells who, having nothing to lose within the system, are thus easily attracted to a movement geared towards overthrowing it.

In regard to the latter point, the generality of terrorist leaders throughout the world, both past and present, appear to have had above average education and have come from the more prosperous end of society (Calvert, 1973). Equally, many current or recent terrorist groups' rank and file, such as the German Baader Meinhof gang, the American Weathermen and the Japanese Red Army are composed largely of intellectuals (Clutterbuck, 1975). In contrast, the Provisional IRA is exceptional in being almost entirely devoid of intellectual elements and contemptuous of what little intellectual support they have had (Clutterbuck, 1975; Laqueur, 1977). The same is true, as far as one can see, of Protestant paramilitary organisations in Northern Ireland.

This is particularly remarkable in the context of the Northern Irish conflict which received much of its initial impetus from politically minded students at Queen's University, Belfast. Inevitably, perhaps, as the initially pure and abstract political theme of civil rights gave way to the more ecologically valid sectarian issues, that intellectual support dwindled to nothing. The intellectual left of both religious persuasions now find themselves in a position not so much in the centre as on a rather high fence above the present conflict.

In regard to the assertion that terrorist groups contain strong psychopathic elements, the argument here tends to be speculative and circular. It is speculative in so far as, to my knowledge, there is no psychological evidence that those who have been involved in terrorist activities are, in fact, diagnosably psychopathic or otherwise clinically disturbed. Indeed, what little evidence there is of this type points in exactly the opposite direction. Elliott and Lockhart (in press) have shown that despite remarkably similar socio-economic backgrounds, juvenile scheduled offenders (broadly, those found guilty of terrorist-related offences) in their particular study were more intelligent, had higher educational attainments, showed less evidence of early developmental problems and had fewer court appearances than 'ordinary' juvenile delinquents.

The argument is also circular since the psychopathic nature of the terrorists is inferred from the sorts of behaviour in which they tend to indulge from time to time. However, since this sort of behaviour, as I have argued, is by no means confined to terrorists and indeed appears to be normal in conflict situations, then the term 'psychopath' is in danger of becoming quite meaningless. What exactly, then, is a psychopath?

The most detailed clinical accounts of psychopathy and its associated behaviours have been given by Cleckley (1964) whose descriptions derive from extensive clinical experience. His outline of the main characteristics is as follows: superficial charm and good intelligence; absence of delusions and other signs of irrational thinking; absence of 'nervousness' or neurotic manifestations; unreliability; untruthfulness and insincerity; lack of remorse or shame; anti-social behaviour without apparent compunction; poor judgment and failure to learn from experience; pathological egocentricity and incapacity for love; general poverty in major affective (emotional) reactions; specific loss of insight; unresponsiveness in general interpersonal relations; fantastic and uninviting behaviour with drink and sometimes without; suicide threats rarely carried out; sex life impersonal, trivial and poorly integrated; failure to follow any life plan.

Although Cleckley's description is fairly comprehensive, other researchers have tried to pinpoint the most crucial features of the psychopath's behaviour. McCord and McCord (1964) consider the two essential features of psychopathy to be 'lovelessness' and 'guiltlessness'. Craft (1965) emphasised lack of feeling, affection or love for others and a tendency to act on impulse and without forethought and both Foulds (1965) and Buss (1966) considered egocentricity and lack of empathy to be key features.

The question arises as to what extent the sorts of descriptions given above can be applied to terrorists in Northern Ireland. The question of extent is not merely one of how many but also of how much because it is a moot point as to whether psychopathy can be considered a quite distinct clinical and behavioural disposition or whether what we conversationally refer to as a psychopathy is, in reality, the extreme end of a dimension such as intelligence along which individuals can be rated as high, medium or low. However, this is not the place for the study of such an issue and we must, as Hare (1970) did, even in a comprehensive analysis of psychopathy, hold the matter in abeyance.

How well do terrorists in Northern Ireland fit the descriptions of psychopaths given above? Although terrorism is fast becoming an area of respectable and serious academic study, it is perhaps unique in that it involves the study of a current phenomenon of human behaviour without any real direct access to the people whose behaviour is being studied. As Mallin (1978) has pointed out, interviews with terrorists are virtually unavailable. However some interviews with Irish terrorists' leaders have been obtained (Sweetman, 1972) and we have the impressions of several Provisional IRA leaders by the Protestant clergy who met them in Feakle in County Clare in December 1974 in a bid for peace (*Sunday Times*, 18 June 1978). Maria McGuire (1973) has written of her experiences during a year's involvement with the leadership of the Provisional IRA and Provisional Sinn Fein, its political wing, although there are claims and counter-claims as to the validity of her views (e.g. MacStiofain, 1975). And Sean MacStiofain (1975), former Chief of Staff of the Provisional IRA, has written an autobiographical account of his involvement in militant Republicanism. We have a very little information on prominent Protestant paramilitaries (e.g. Boulton, 1973) and of the rank and file of either Protestant or Catholic terrorist groups we know virtually nothing although Burton (1978) has some valuable information and insights into the reality of rank and file IRA membership in a Belfast Catholic community in the 1972-73 period.

Of the leadership of terrorist organisations as portrayed in these various accounts, it is fair to say that none even remotely resemble either the popular image of a psychopath or the more precise and detailed clinical descriptions given by the clinicians mentioned above. The comment by journalists John Whale and Chris Ryder on the Provisional IRA leadership at the Feakle talks is a fair summary: 'Their dedication verged on the puritanical. "We thought", said one of the clerics, "they'd be hard-living, hard drinking morons." In fact, whereas all the ministers drank alcohol except one, only one Provisional did, and none smoked except O'Connell'. (*Sunday Times*, 18 June 1978) Psychopaths, in contrast, are dedicated only to themselves.

Sean MacStiofain perhaps best fits the popular stereotype of a terrorist and, indeed, has been described as 'the only real terrorist' the IRA has ever succeeded in producing. Certainly, there is an extra fanatical tinge to his dedication, fuelled possibly by self-perceived flaws in his Irishness (his father was English, he was born and brought up as John Stephenson in England and served in the Royal Air Force) and in the purity of his Catholic background (his mother was married twice and his father, a heavy drinker, remarried within a year of his mother's death when he was ten). He seems, by his own autobiographical account, to have been a difficult and contentious young man given to expressing his opinions when silence would have made life easier (a characteristic incompatible with psychopathy).

His predominant personality feature appears to be authoritarianism coupled with a fanatical dedication to the cause of a United Ireland free from Britain. This comes across much more strongly in his interview with Sweetman (1972) when he was Chief of Staff than in his autobiography, written when he had fallen from grace in the Republican movement as a result of his failure to continue a hunger and thirst strike in an Irish prison. For example, Sweetman (1972) records him as saying 'I can't see any place for Craig and his type in a United Ireland. There would be no place for those who say they want their British heritage. They've got to accept their Irish heritage, and the Irish way of life, no matter who they are, otherwise there would be no place for them' (p. 157).

Although authoritarianism and fanaticism are still evident, sometimes just below the surface, in his autobiography, they are leavened by the expression of some quite distinctly 'soft' attitudes. For example, he expresses affection for the English working classes and countryside, regret for the death of individual soldiers, and admiration for aspects of English penal policy, amongst other things. Presumably, with the role requirements of terrorist leader lifted from him, his autobiographical disclosures could afford to be less fanatical. In any case, authoritarianism is not psychopathy and fanatical dedication to a cause is quite inconsistent with the psychopathic personality.

Burton (1978), an English academic sociologist, reports on his experiences of living for eight months during the period 1972-73 in a Belfast Catholic community in which the IRA was active. His analysis is unique in that we have no other information on such a community from a disinterested source based on such prolonged and intimate contact. Despite the fact that the protracted gap between the study and his report of it in his book in many respects renders it of historical interest rather than current relevance, his comments on the personal characteristics of the terrorists with whom he came into contact are of great importance, particularly in view of our relative ignorance of rank and file terrorists.

Burton argues that much of the sort of behaviour which outsiders tend to conceptualise as typical of the evil or psychopathic nature of members of the Provisional IRA was, in fact, quite differently construed inside the community. For example, the harsh and summary punishments meted out to offenders (such as knee-capping and tarring and feathering) were seen by those within Burton's community in the context of repressive British laws, brutal and illegal enforcement by British troops and differential treatment of the two communities. Burton is particularly revealing, from personal experience, on the ferocious behaviour of British troops, particularly the Paratroop Regiment, towards the inhabitants of the community in which he lived. The following extract speaks for itself :

'. . . A discotheque was interrupted by a foot-patrol who attacked the teenage dancers, putting one boy back into the hospital from which he had just been released. He had the stitches from a routine operation on his stomach reopened by the troops. A baker's hand was broken by the soldiers as he went about his delivery round. A store of furniture belonging to homeless, intimidated families was wrecked during a search. Local mill workers were kicked in the genitals as they were searched, twice daily, as they went to and from their workplace. I was hit in the ribs as two Paratroopers asked me if I was in the IRA. I said that I was not and they replied, "Well, fucking well join so that we can shoot you." The friend I was living with was beaten up in the back of a Saracen tank by a Paratroop sergeant. After being interrogated and cleared he was taken back to Anro [the pseudonym given by Burton to his community] by the same soldier who apologised, "I'm sorry about that lad on the way down, we do it to everyone. People soon start talking after we soften them up." In addition to these and hosts of other examples, four people were shot dead in heatedly disputed circumstances.' (p. 107)

In these circumstances, the Provisionals' kangaroo courts and rough justice merely parallelled the activities of the British government and its security forces. Indeed, as Burton notes, when the customary appeals to the Catholic community to 'reject the men of violence' were made, they were accepted. The community rejected them in the form of the British Army. In the intervening years since Burton's study, which was carried out at the height of the present troubles, this attitude may well have mellowed as the Army gradually took on a lower profile over the years. But some residue, at least, of this feeling probably remains.

As for the character of the typical Provisional IRA members, Burton records an inability to typify them as a group, although he does note a common and pervasive authoritarianism among them, a characteristic noted of Sean MacStiofain. He makes the point, which carries considerable weight, that if the picture of the Provisional IRA as woven by the media and government propagandists were true, he and his two English companions with whom he lived in this militant area, would not have survived.

Although Burton does describe a proportion of Provisional volunteers as young 'yahoo' or 'hood' elements of the sort which most nearly matches the public image, he notes that even these were not a uniform type. Some, apparently, were still 'wild men' but others, who had been villains prior to their involvement, had become 'politicised by the IRA and straightened out of their non-political violence' (p. 117). Burton claims that bouts of depression, self-doubt and guilt were common among active IRA men and that he saw little evidence of the criminal racketeering of which the Provisionals have been accused. Indeed, dedication and material sacrifice appeared to attend Provisional involvement normally. It is of interest, however, that he describes a Provisional who deliberately maintained a psychopathic 'front' to protect himself from doubt and fear. He refused the IRA wage 'on principle', never had any money, realised that he had only a short time to live and indeed was shot dead by a British Army Paratrooper shortly after having his memory cards printed. Despite the image, this does not seem like psychopathic behaviour.

Storr (1978) has made the point that while aggression is a feature of the behaviour of many species, cruelty seems peculiar to humans and normal people have the potential for violent and cruel behaviour. He argues, as I have argued here, that since psychopaths constitute such a small proportion of human beings, it is inappropriate to explain cruel behaviour away as being solely or even predominantly perpetrated by psychopathic individuals.

To argue that the Provisional IRA is not an organisation of psychopaths (which is, incidentally, a contradiction in terms in view of the psychopath's difficulties in maintaining trusting and lasting relationships) is not, of course, to argue that there are no psychopathic individuals in such organisations. Conflict-oriented groups, it seems reasonable to assume, will attract certain types of individual. It is difficult to imagine, for example, a young man tossing a coin to decide whether to join the clergy or the SAS. These are not totally random choices. Psychopathic individuals may be attracted to conflict-oriented groups to indulge themselves with impunity, and indeed, in the short-term, may be useful to such organisations for the perpetration of acts at which more normal individuals might baulk. In the long-term, however, their egocentricity and unreliability would make them a dangerous liability to such an organisation and it is unlikely that any would be given responsibility or leadership within a rational conflict-oriented group.

Authoritarian individuals are also likely to be attracted to conflict-oriented groups by the formal and delineated structure of the organisation (in those cases, such as the Provisional IRA and the British Army which have a formal structure) and by the opportunity to exercise authority both within the group and, as a result of its activities, in a wider sphere of society at large. Indeed if one were pressed to give the single most likely characteristic of the terrorist (or indeed of any member of a conflict-oriented group) then, on the basis of the evidence to hand, authoritarianism appears to be the most generally distributed personality attribute. It is interesting to note that the Official IRA, which has been in a state of cease-fire for several years, is led by Cathal Goulding, a very easy-going and non-authoritarian individual (Sweetman, 1972).

The population from which terrorists are drawn will be those who genuinely believe in the aims of the group, those who are attracted by the glamour of membership which, according to Burton (1978), was a considerable proportion of young men in his community, those who are bored, with nothing better to do and those who are looking for a measure of excitement in life (or some combination of these motives). Again, one is not arguing that all terrorists are authoritarian, but the combination of authoritarianism with one of these sources of motivation will probably increase the chances of an individual's joining and remaining within a terrorist group.

In the Irish context two features of this scenario are of particular interest. The first is authoritarianism which is a personality characteristic which predisposes the individual to a coherent cluster of conservative, right-wing attitudes which, although sharing certain characteristics across cultures, may vary between cultures according to the specific social, religious and political traditions. Roger Brown (1965) gives an excellent analysis of the research behind this concept and of the failure to date, of researchers to find a corresponding 'authoritarianism of the left' of the sort which might account, for example, for hard-line communist views.

Ireland, both North and South, is a traditionalist and conservative country both politically and religiously. People are raised with traditional and conservative political and religious values. One might, therefore, expect to find a somewhat higher incidence of authoritarianism in Ireland than in England, for example. As I have argued, the context will, to some extent, determine the specific content of the cluster of attitudes to which this disposition gives rise and two authoritarian individuals may hold diametrically opposed specific views. For example, an authoritarian Protestant may have an unyielding attitude towards remaining within the United Kingdom while an authoritarian Catholic may implacably be committed to a United Ireland independent of Britain. Both, however, will probably have similar views on the appropriate treatment of (non-political) offenders, sex before marriage, the importance of religion and so forth.

The second feature which is important in terms of attitudes towards conflict-oriented groups is the question of motivation. In Ireland, there is a historical legitimacy attributed to taking up arms in the defence of one's heritage and, explicitly in the Republican tradition, a cultural exaltation of armed conflict of the guerilla type. The IRA has a long and, in the main, honourable tradition of nationalist struggle against British occupation and one would, therefore, expect to find, in the Catholic population, a not inconsiderable proportion of people brought up to respect the general ideals of Irish nationalism and sympathetic to the traditional, guerilla means of attaining it. It is, in fact, not quite so absurd to imagine a young Irishman tossing up a coin to decide whether to join the priesthood or the IRA. In addition, with the high rate of unemployment in Northern Ireland, particularly in Catholic areas, one would expect a higher than usual motivation to escape boredom.

Although there is a traditional respect for the force of arms in the Northern Protestant tradition, there is no widespread tradition of guerilla warfare and, interestingly, it is from the ranks of the Protestant paramilitary groups that the preponderance of truly psychopathic terrorist activity has emanated, with the random and frequently grisly assassinations of Catholics. The recent 'Shankill butcher' trials have revealed details of this sort of psychopathic behaviour, which can flourish somewhat more easily in organisations which lack the cultural traditions and historical respectability of the IRA and hence do not tend so readily to attract the stabilising element nurtured on those traditions and conscious to some extent, at least, of the ideals behind the conflict.

D

The same arguments would apply to any conflict-oriented group whose aims are somewhat diffuse. It is difficult to imagine that the typical soldier in the British Army has any burning desire to maintain Ulster as an integral part of the United Kingdom. Nor, for that matter, can one imagine that the average recruit has any real commitment to the defence of the West in a major conflict. For the majority, the motivations will be a secure job, an escape from unemployment, and an opportunity for travel and excitement. The British Army will also have its quota of the psychopathic and authoritarian and it is arguable that this proportion may be higher than in the IRA, given the suggested lack of felt ideals which the recruit might realise by joining up.

It is important to stress the relative clarity of ideals at this point for it is not at all clear what the ultimate objectives of the Provisional IRA actually are or indeed if they have any specific and remotely obtainable goals which would conceivably be acceptable to the people of Ireland, Catholic or Protestant, North or South. However, they are committed, in admittedly vague and unrealistic terms, to a United Ireland free of British influence and that, for all its woolly-headedness, is a rather more clear and concrete objective than the aims of many conflict-oriented groups, including the British Army.

I have argued here that the behaviour of terrorists cannot be attributed, in any significant degree, to their psychopathic nature. In Chapter Six we shall see that both the Republic of Ireland and Northern Ireland are areas where relatively low levels of crime and delinquency have been and still are the norm in comparison, for example, to England and Wales. On this basis, we might reasonably assume that psychopathic behaviour has not been a feature of life in Northern Ireland which has merely found a haven in terrorist activity.

Authoritarianism, which appears to characterise many terrorists, is not an abnormal condition, indeed it is quite a common characteristic within the population and does not per se predispose people to the sorts of atrocious behaviour in which terrorists indulge. The task, therefore, remains of specifying the circumstances in which otherwise normal people can indulge in this sort of behaviour and in order to do that we must diverge briefly into experimental social psychology.

Research by Stanley Milgram (1974) in the United States has shown very clearly that ordinary individuals are quite capable of very cruel behaviour in the right circumstances. Milgram set up a situation in which people were paid to participate in what they believed was an experimental investigation of the effects of punishment on learning. Each subject was introduced to his partner subject who, in fact, was a 'stooge' or confederate of the experimenter, and they drew lots to determine who was going to be the teacher and who the learner in the experimental situation. This procedure was rigged so that the confederate always became the learner.

The task of the teacher was to punish incorrect responses by the learner in a learning task. The learner was strapped into a chair with an electrode on his wrist. Punishment was to be administered by an impressive apparatus which sent electric shocks to the learner. The apparatus contained thirty switches which enabled the teacher to administer shocks of increasing severity to the learner each time he made an error on the learning task. The switches were marked at 15 volt intervals up to 450 volts and were clearly labelled at levels from 'Slight Shock' up to 'Danger: Extreme Shock' and finally an ominous 'XXX'.

The experimenter informed the subject that 'although the shocks can be extremely painful, they cause no permanent tissue damage' and to give the subject or teacher an idea of what a slight shock felt like, he was given a sample of 45 volts. This was the only shock actually administered in the entire procedure. The learner received no shocks at all, although the teacher did not know this.

The situation was arranged so that the learner made many errors in the learning task, so requiring the teacher to move progressively up the voltage scale of punishment shocks. If the teacher questioned the wisdom or desirability of the procedure at any point, the experimenter, who was standing nearby, simply replied that 'The experiment requires that you continue' or 'You have no other choice; you must go on'.

The experiment was conducted under a variety of conditions. In one condition, the learner was in a separate room from the teacher (the learner responded by pressing one of four switches which lit corresponding lights on the teacher's control panel). At 150 volts the learner showed his pain by shouting 'Experimenter, get me out of here! I refuse to go on!' At 180 volts he shouted that he found the pain unbearable and at 270 volts gave an agonised scream. At 300 he pounded on the wall separating his room from the teacher's and thereafter made no further response. Under these conditions 62·5 per cent of subjects carried on to shocking the learner right up to 450 volts.

In another condition, the learner (who gave an absolutely convincing performance, as film of the experiment shows) was actually in the same room as the teacher and in these circumstances 40 per cent of subjects carried on to the highest level of shock despite the visible and audible evidence of the learner's distress. In yet another condition, the teacher was obliged after the 150 volt level to physically force the learner's unwilling hand onto a shock plate in order to deliver punishment. Even under these circumstances, 30 per cent of subjects carried on to 450 volts.

It should be stressed that Milgram's subjects were ordinary people and not sadists. To check that the behaviour of subjects would not be so callous and cruel without the authority of the experimenter, Milgram set up a control experiment in which subjects could choose their own levels of shock. These were selected almost entirely from the lower ranges of the shock control board.

Milgram himself was astounded at the results of his experiments. The most cynical estimate he obtained prior to his study was that about 3 per cent of subjects would obey throughout whereas, in the event, up to 65 per cent delivered the maximum shock and all subjects obeyed up to 300 volts. In one of the many variations of the experimental situation where subjects were only required to perform a subsidiary role (reading the words the learner was required to learn), 90 per cent stayed with the experiment right through to the 450 volts level. Kilham and Mann (1974) confirmed this tendency in a replication of Milgram's experiment, finding that subjects only required to give the order to someone else to shock the learner were more compliant.

So here we have a startling demonstration of the degree to which ordinary people will behave callously, harshly and cruelly against an innocent victim who has done them no harm simply on the say-so of an experimenter in a psychological experiment. It should be noted that at no time did the experimenter threaten the subject with any consequences of his disobedience but merely asserted his authority in the vaguest possible terms ('The experiment requires that you continue.') The subjects ascribed to the experimenter an authority which he did not, in fact, possess.

I have argued throughout this chapter that judging the character of others simply on the basis of their overt behaviour is highly misleading. Milgram's subjects, however, made the complementary error of judging their own behaviour on the basis of their feelings about what they were doing as it was happening. Many were clearly very distressed during the experiment and in the debriefing session after each experiment in which everything was explained to the subject, many took consolation from their feelings of disgust and sympathy during the experiment. Such sentiments, of course, would have been of little use to their victims if, as they believed, he was actually suffering the pain and distress which they were inflicting.

A revealing experiment by Zimbardo and his associates (1973) also gives us pause to reflect from a somewhat different angle, on the stability of the standards of behaviour to which most of us would lay claim. Zimbardo, who was investigating the effects of roles on behaviour, set up a situation in which a group of university students were to live for a short period as prison guards and prisoners. As the situation developed, a very dramatic change in the behaviour and outlook of both 'prisoner' and 'guards' began to take place. 'Prisoners' became more withdrawn and emotionally distressed and 'guards' became more punitive and authoritarian. In fact, the situation reached such a pitch that Zimbardo and his co-workers had to call off the experiment before its scheduled finish to avoid any possible harm or distress to his subjects, who had become so involved in their roles that the roles had begun to take over from the reality. Of particular interest, from the perspective of this chapter, is the behaviour of the 'prison guards' whose roles occasioned them to behave harshly and callously even though they were normal young men.

It is in the light of such experimental evidence that one can begin to understand the behaviour which typifies conflict-oriented groups in general and terrorist organisations such as the Provisional IRA in particular. We have noted Storr's (1978) point that aggression is a human characteristic and that, uniquely among the species, cruelty is within all human beings. We should also note that conflict-oriented groups, such as the Provisional

IRA or the British Army are organisations based on the premise that force or violence, or at the very least the threat of force or violence, is instrumental in obtaining certain objectives. Fine sociological distinctions between force (legitimate) and violence (illegitimate) make little psychological sense since, as we have seen, legitimacy is in the eye of the beholder and a corpse is a corpse. Violence is what you use on me, force what I use on you.

Conflict-oriented groups, therefore, are organisations designed to elicit from men (and women) the potential for aggression and cruelty which they clearly possess and to supply them with the means for maximising the effect of that aggression and cruelty. This aggression and cruelty is normally kept in check by society's norms of appropriate behaviour and the system of formal and informal sanctions on those who transgress such norms. So how do people break the grip of those norms and the effects of years of social training inculcating such values as kindness and consideration for others? Milgram (1974) has suggested some interesting reasons why his subjects behaved as they did.

First, Milgram proposes that the experimental situation had inherent 'binding factors' such as politeness to the experimenter, the obligation to fulfil a promise to participate and the awkwardness and embarrassment of withdrawal. Ironically, the very social norms that would usually prevent one from harming someone, Milgram suggests, actually prevent one from not harming someone.

Second, Milgram proposes that there were 'adjustment factors' which served to distance the subject from the effects of his behaviour on his victim. Subjects became involved in the technical aspects of their task, tried to be competent at it, attributed the responsibility for the proceedings to the experimenter and hence their moral concern correspondingly diminished. Moreover, in a process fearsomely titled 'counteranthropomorphism', they tended to deny the human element in what was an institutionalised procedure; they suppressed their normal reactions to distress in others in the name of experimentation or scientific enquiry. The quintessential example of counteranthropomorphism in everyday life would be the attitude of the public executioner or, in these more 'enlightened' times, the attitude of the judge in sentencing a convicted man to prolonged imprisonment.

Milgram's findings and suggested explanations of them give

us pause to think about our current conceptions of 'evil' and 'evil men'. Clearly, in situations where men perceive themselves to be under authority, even if that authority is vague, a remarkable proportion will obey the command to hurt and distress others. Hannah Arendt (1963), writing of the Eichmann trials in Jerusalem, has questioned the validity of the prosecution's effort to depict Eichmann as a sadistic fiend. Rather, she saw him as a desk-bound bureaucrat doing a job and commented upon the 'banality of evil'. Certainly, Milgram's analysis tends to support that conceptualisation.

If one looks at conflict-oriented groups, it is clear that they are unique in the degree to which they are structured and the emphasis which they place on authority and pecking order. While other sorts of organisations, for example in industry, have tended to move away from an authority-bound approach towards a more co-operative ambience, military organisations continue to stress authority and formality. That fact is not just a reflection of the love of military organisations for tradition, but rather a recognition that authority and organised violence are inextricably linked.

Milgram's research has brought to light and subjected to theoretical analysis a phenomenon of human behaviour with which military practitioners have been familiar for centuries. All the square-bashing, saluting, kit-cleaning and endless, apparently pointless regimentation and authority is geared towards the day when vile acts and atrocious behaviour will be called for and received.

We usually tend to think that death and destruction are the business of armies other than our own and particularly the business of our enemies. But death and destruction, or the threat of death and destruction (which can only be a real threat if one can actually kill and destroy) is the very stuff of any conflict-oriented group. And the ability to deliver these goods effectively in any sizeable organisation is dependent upon the clear and unequivocal establishment of authority and obedience. Only in these circumstances will otherwise normal men truncheon, rifle-butt, shoot, stab and bomb complete strangers and ransack and destroy their property. Milgram's analysis has suggested to us the psychological means by which men can do these things and live with themselves during and after the event.

Transplanting this argument to the IRA, it is not by accident that the command structure of the IRA is so formalised. David Blundy has described the extremely stiff and formalised meetings of the Provisional Army Council in which military discipline is the norm, Christian names are banned and members are addressed by their full paramilitary titles despite long acquaintance and close friendship within the group (*Sunday Times*, 3 July 1977). New recruits to the IRA enter a formalised structure in which orders are given, obedience demanded and disobedience punished harshly.

Within this relationship of obedient member to authoritarian structure, it begins to come clear how the terrorist can cope with the awesome responsibility of his deeds. He too will be subject to binding factors even if the reality of his membership proves less palatable than the expectation. For example, he will feel obliged to fulfil the commitment of his membership. It would be awkward and embarrassing (not to mention, possibly dangerous) for him to get out. Equally, he will have technical and practical aspects of his activities on which to focus and so diminish his moral concern. For example, he may be called upon to gather explosive substances, construct explosive devices, avoid the attentions of the security forces and so on. And he too will be prone to engage in counteranthropomorphism in the name of Irish liberation, freedom from British rule and so forth.

Not only will the new recruit have entered a formal structure, he will also have entered a role which will make specific demands on his attitudes and behaviour. The role is one of 'guerilla', 'freedom fighter', 'revolutionary' or the role favoured and promoted by the Republican movement, 'soldier-politician' (Burton, 1978). This promotion is deliberately undertaken to counter the imputation of the more current label which I have used throughout this chapter, namely 'terrorist'. The requirements of the role of Provisional IRA member are many and varied—toughness, courage, ruthlessness, daring, planter of bombs, killer of soldiers and so forth. And, as Zimbardo's work has demonstrated, roles can powerfully affect how we behave and how we perceive ourselves.

Above all, perhaps, the Provisional IRA man's role is that of perpetrator of deeds, especially deeds of violence and destruction. The political element of the role is very much the poor relation and, as Burton (1978) notes, the experiences undergone by Provisionals during a protracted and ugly conflict tend to make them mistake political compromise for treachery, an insult to their dead and to the suffering of their communities. Having accepted the role of freedom fighter or soldier-politician, and thus measuring one's role success in terms of violent and certainly visible action, the difficulty arises of getting off what has become a self-propelled roundabout. Action equals strength, strength equals success and success equals action. As Laqueur (1977) notes 'Terrorism in any case is not a philosophical school—it is always the action that counts'. Some commentators feel that the perfect time for switching from a military to a political role was in the spring and summer of 1972 when the British government abolished Stormont and negotiated directly with the Provisionals. As Whale (1973) commented, 'Instead of turning their chips into money when they could, they staked them on another throw; and they lost the lot' (p. 6).

And so a psychological framework emerges capable of explaining much of the phenomenon of terrorism in Ireland without significant recourse to such concepts as psychopathic or evil behaviour which, in reality, provide only labels and not explanation, only moral sticks and not understanding. By a process of inference, I have argued that the behaviour of terrorists does not differ substantially from the behaviour of men in conflict-oriented groups generally, and that behaviour is largely explicable, at a psychological level, in terms of the formalistic and authoritarian structure of conflict-oriented groups and the role requirements of members of such groups. Furthermore, I have endeavoured to show that similar behaviour can be elicited from ordinary people in the right circumstances.

I have attempted, in short, to show that the behaviour of terrorists can be encompassed in the sweep of current social psychological theory. I have tried to avoid becoming ensnared in moralistic and, from my perspective, ultimately counter-productive stances. This should not be taken as indicative of a personal indifference to the morality of terrorist activity, for nothing could be further from the truth. However, above all I have tried to keep in mind that most of the people who have been or still are or will be involved in terrorist activity will ultimately return or be returned to the Northern Irish community. If this analysis in any way facilitates that process, it will have achieved its objective.
    D*

CHAPTER FIVE

Leadership

This chapter will attempt to look at leadership in Ulster utilising the framework of leadership which has emerged in psychological research. The primary emphasis will be on Protestant leaders since it is they who have had the main responsibility of rearing 'the unwanted baby' (Cole, 1969) of Ulster even though its real parents, the British government under Lloyd George, dumped a genetically defective child on their doorstep. This emphasis should not be taken to indicate any derogation of Catholic leadership nor, indeed, should it be interpreted as implying that the responsibility for all of Ulster's ills lies exclusively with the Protestant/Unionist side. However, Protestant leaders have had the responsibility of providing leadership not only for the majority Protestant community, but as government ministers over the years, for the Northern Irish community as a whole, both Catholic and Protestant. Apart from the brief life-span of the power-sharing Northern Ireland Executive, this responsibility has not fallen to Catholic leaders.

In dealing with the question of leadership in Northern Ireland as a whole, therefore, one inevitably must concentrate on Protestant leaders. Implicit in this orientation is the view that the eventual form of solution to the present impasse in Northern Ireland will be determined more critically by developments in the Protestant community than by developments elsewhere in Ulster or beyond. It is the Protestants, at the end of the day, who form the clear democratic majority in Northern Ireland. Without substantial Catholic consensus, future political developments would be fraught with difficulty; without substantial Protestant consensus, they would be impossible.

Leadership Research

The history of leadership research in the social sciences is characterised by somewhat overwrought and simplistic concepts of leadership which have tended to yield disappointing results and unsatisfactory analyses.

Early research assumed a 'great man' model of leadership and endeavoured to enumerate those personal qualities which leaders in a wide variety of situations possess. The results were inconsistent, although a few qualities, such as intelligence, had some generality, more often than not, no relationship was found between a given characteristic and leadership (Stogdill, 1948; Mann, 1959). It is interesting to note that this model of leadership has currency in Northern Ireland. Rose (1971) found in his survey that 65 per cent of his respondents agreed with the proposition that 'some people are born to rule'. This was a dominant view in both communities, 70 per cent of Protestants and 59 per cent of Catholics agreeing. The characteristic presumably felt to underline this born ability is not altogether clear, although one might surmise that it is something to do with intelligence or an ability to see the larger perspective since the majority of respondents (65 per cent Protestant and 66 per cent Catholic) thought that 'people with the most education are best to govern the country'.

As a reaction against the paucity of useful results in this line of research (and, to some extent, against the ethos underlying it) the focus of research in the 1950s was on the particular circumstances which brought a leader to the fore in a given situation. Sometimes referred to as 'social forces theory', the situation was regarded as the dominant influence on events, leaders emerging inevitably, and somewhat mysteriously, to sit atop a rushing wave of circumstance.

Both views were overstated and it is now recognised that while particular situations demand particular leadership qualities, some people are more suitable than others to fill any given leadership role (Fiedler, 1965; Gibb, 1969).

Recent analyses have been much more realistic in their recognition of the importance of followers in the total picture of a leadership situation and have emphasised the continual transactional nature of leader-follower relationships (Sanford, 1950; Homans, 1961; Hollander and Julian, 1969; Hollander, 1976).

This sort of analysis is particularly appropriate for understanding the nature of democratic leadership in the political world, where followers have various institutionalised forms of sanction on leadership, especially at election times.

Bales and Slater (1955) first articulated clearly an important differentiation in the concept of leadership, namely between the 'task specialist' and the 'social emotional specialist'. The former is the man who gets things done while the latter is the one who pours oil on the troubled waters of the task specialist's wake and keeps the group functioning smoothly and harmoniously. However, while Bales and Slater have demonstrated that those two roles are often occupied by different persons in laboratory group endeavours, there is no necessary conflict between the roles (Marcus, 1960; Turk, 1961) and it is unlikely that modern political leaders could remain in office for long while being completely deficient in one or other respects (Elms, 1976).

Despite the general validity of Elms' point, it is possible to exemplify political leaders who are relatively stronger on one aspect of leadership rather than the other (without implying any judgment on the absolute levels of either). In the recent past of the United States, for example, it can be argued that President Kennedy's forte was social-emotional leadership while the present incumbent, President Carter is primarily a task specialist. In British politics, the respective counterparts would be Harold Wilson (social-emotional) and Edward Heath (task). In the politics of Northern Ireland, Terence O'Neill was stronger on social-emotional leadership (although he was ultimately unsuccessful in its application) while Brian Faulkner was clearly a task specialist.

However, not only is it unlikely that political leaders can be completely deficient in one of the two theoretical aspects of leadership, but in politics the line between the two is often invisible. Nowhere is this more so than in Northern Ireland. For example, O'Neill's social-emotional leadership inevitably entailed the accomplishment of certain political tasks, namely legislation to remove the disadvantages of the Catholic population. The former makes no sense without the latter. And it was, to some extent at least, the failure of O'Neill's task leadership to keep pace with his social-emotional leadership which formed the vacuum in which the present troubles erupted. Equally, Brian Faulkner's ultimate political demise indicates that even consummate skill in task accomplishment without a corresponding social-emotional relationship are similarly unproductive, in Ulster politics at least.

A related factor in terms of political leadership is the perceived legitimacy of leadership. Burke (1972) for example, has shown that in the laboratory, when the emergent leader of a small group is legitimised in the sense that there is a consensus that the task he is trying to accomplish is important and appropriate for the group as a whole, then no clear differentiation develops between task-oriented and social-emotional roles. Few of us, trapped in a burning building, would mind being hustled unceremoniously to safety.

Hollander and Julian (1970) have demonstrated by cleverly contrived laboratory experiments that elected, rather than appointed leaders of small groups can be tough taskmasters at the expense of social-emotional leadership and can more effectively pursue their own course against the wishes of their followers, particularly when the margin by which they are elected is large.

These findings are particularly relevant to the course of Terence O'Neill's career as Prime Minister. It is difficult to divine what the exact circumstances of his appointment were. Apparently, there was an understanding between Prime Minister Brookeborough and back-benchers that the new leader would eventually be chosen at a formal meeting of the Parliamentary Party (Harbinson, 1973). However, Brookeborough appears to have given O'Neill the impression that he recommended him alone to the Governor although O'Neill (1972) claims that the Governor subsequently told him that Brookeborough refused to recommend anyone. Another version of the story is that Brookeborough recommended three names to the Governor (O'Neill, Faulkner and Andrews) and asked him to make his choice (Bleakley, 1974). And finally, several authors claim that William Craig, as Chief Whip, was the key figure in the appointment, garnered support for O'Neill for his own ends, held a straw poll over the telephone after Brookeborough's resignation and advised the Governor accordingly (e.g. Boyd, 1972; Harbinson, 1973; Devlin, 1975).

Whatever the truth of the matter and whatever the circumstances surrounding it (Brian Faulkner, an obvious choice and

O'Neill's main rival, for example, was in the United States at the time), there was considerable resentment in the Unionist Party that O'Neill had been foisted upon them. It is, therefore, possible to argue that his subsequent difficulties might never have arisen had he been properly elected, although many feel that Brian Faulkner might have won such an election. The Unionist Party would then have been under pressure to justify their decision by backing O'Neill's policies more strongly than they did and, as Hollander and Julian's (1970) findings indicate, he would arguably have found less resistance in pursuing his own course within the party if he had been properly elected.

Leaders and Followers in Ulster

The problem of democratic political leadership is how to reconcile the diverse interests and aspirations of a community with the most important interests and aspirations of the majority of that community by whose votes one was elected. The diversity of issues in general elections and the inability of any party to continually fulfil all of those aspirations usually ensures electoral defeat for a governing party sooner or later in Western democracies.

In Northern Ireland, however, there never was a range of issues of sufficient importance to the electorate to cause a change of government from the Unionist Party which continually ruled the country from 1921-1972. Throughout that period there was only one electoral issue and that was whether Northern Ireland would remain within the United Kingdom as opposed to uniting with the Irish Republic. There was, therefore, no real need to engage in further political discussion since Unionist leaders could always, in the final analysis, sidetrack opposition criticism into the issue of sovereignty. It was not always necessary to do even this since criticism was frequently couched in aggressively nationalist or republican terms. Because the major alternative to Unionist rule was Nationalist/Republican rule and the disintegration of Northern Ireland, opposition criticism was, at best, viewed as self-interested and, at worst, practically treasonable.

So the Unionist leadership in Northern Ireland basically defined its goal as preventing the Nationalist opposition and the almost exclusively Catholic minority which they represented from having their political will. Reduced to its crudest and simplest, Unionists won elections on the basis of what they had not done and would not do (join a United Ireland) rather than on the basis of what they had achieved and would achieve in the future (which is not to say that they did not achieve anything). Perhaps more importantly, however, successive generations of Unionist leaders defined the Catholic population out of their followership, only one of many possible illustrations being Craigavon's infamous statement that Stormont was 'a Protestant Parliament for a Protestant people'.

Thus, the Unionist leadership effectively avoided the effort and burden of leadership by seeking only to please the Protestant section of the community and, at that, choosing to devote its prime energy to only one aspect of government, namely the maintenance of the constitutional position. To gild the (Orange) lily, the machiavellian touch of actually encouraging distance and enmity between the two communities to perpetuate their power was added. This is illustrated, for example, by Brooke's speech on the 13 July 1933 in which he said '. . . I recommend those people who are loyalists not to employ Roman Catholics, 90 per cent of whom are disloyal. . . . If you don't act properly now, before we know where we are we shall find ourselves in the minority instead of the majority.'

The transactional view of leadership sees rewards and costs on both sides of the leader-follower relationship. For the Protestants the rewards were 'a Protestant Parliament for a Protestant people', resounding victories at elections, triumphant parades through the streets at celebration times and the satisfaction of thinking that they were somehow better off than their Catholic neighbours. Rose's (1971) survey, however found that, overall, Protestants had only a slight income advantage over Catholics, although educated Catholics were proportionately somewhat worse off than their Protestant counterparts. Barritt and Carter's (1972) data on the proportion of Catholics in senior positions in the Northern Ireland Civil Service, for example, is consistent with Rose's findings. However, Aunger's (1975) analysis makes the point that Protestants have been disproportionately represented in the higher-status industries such as shipbuilding and engineering.

The only substantive area where anti-Catholic discriminatory powers were wielded with any enthusiasm to general Protestant

advantage was in political rights. By rigging the electoral boundaries and maintaining the restricted local government franchise,
Catholics were prevented from controlling areas in which they
formed the majority. Londonderry is the worst example of this
practice where, in an area 70 per cent Catholic, Unionists had
50 per cent more representatives than non-Unionists on the
Council, although there are many such examples. Lurgan, for
example had 46 per cent Catholic population with no non-
Unionist representatives whatsoever (Birrell, 1972).

This was an indirect way of giving an economic advantage to
Protestants since discrimination in employment was taken for
granted by many Protestant and Catholic controlled local coun-
cils in Northern Ireland (Barritt and Carter, 1972). But the
political gains made by the Unionist Party as a result of these
measures puts them outside the realm of philanthropy.

The net cost to the Unionist leadership of their transaction
with their Protestant followers was perpetual alienation from the
Catholic third of the population of Northern Ireland; an intract-
able followership reared on the myopic illusion of the indefinite
ability of its leaders to prevent the inevitable alignment of Northern Irish affairs with the standards applicable elsewhere in the
United Kingdom and, ultimately, their own political destruction
when that fragile illusion was shattered by the suspension of
Stormont in March 1972.

The Politics of Paranoia

In fact, what had been created in Northern Ireland was not
a democracy but a 'paranocracy' in which the basis of power
was the successful appeal to paranoid fears in the Protestant
electorate about the political, social, philosophical and military
potential of their Catholic neighbours. Of course, the Unionists
did not invent the paranocracy, nor did they create the most
awesome and horrible version of it, but they are in the same
political tradition as Hitler and McCarthy in the creation and
maintenance of paranoid and irrational fears in one section of
their population about another section of that population.

Politicians, of course, constantly endeavour to exploit public
fears and misapprehensions about certain sections of the community. In Britain, for example, the Conservative Party exploits
public fears about the power of trade unions while the Labour

Party exploits public fears about the greed and power of big business. However this situation does not constitute a paranocracy since (*a*) the criticism is directed at institutions and not at individuals and (*b*) the methods proposed by either side to deal with the perceived problems are objectively moderate. In contrast, the National Front in Britain, with its heavy-handed racist philosophy, would, if popularly supported to any significant extent, create a paranocracy.

Paranoid politics arise with reasonable frequency in otherwise normal countries besides Northern Ireland. Senator McCarthy, for example, briefly converted the United States to a paranocracy by successfully exploiting popular fears and misconceptions about the nature and power of Communism to his political advantage. Hofstader's (1965) book entitled *The Paranoid Style in American Politics* provides further evidence of this phenomenon in the United States. Even in relatively cocooned environments it appears that a paranoid outlook can be a political advantage. Rutherford (1966), in a study of Elgin State Hospital, Illinois, a progressive psychiatric hospital which offers patients considerable responsibility for guiding their own affairs within the hospital, shows that 45·8 per cent of the elected ward councillors were paranoid schizophrenics, although only 11·8 per cent of the ward population were so diagnosed.

Studies of prejudice show that irrational fears of and antagonisms towards minorities are often inflamed by real local difficulties, such as economic hardship (Allport, 1954). And a genuinely perceived threat does appear to provide the best possible circumstances for a paranocracy to grow and gain strength. However, it was the constant and real fragility of the Northern Irish state, underlined by the continuing claims to sovereignty of successive Dublin governments, which provided the sustaining force of the Northern Irish paranocracy.

In the relatively mild and insulated form of paranocracy extant in Northern Ireland, the system became virtually self-sufficient, impervious to economic and social failure, impervious to logical and political rebuttal, and fuelled simply by regular doses of paranoia at appropriate moments in the social and political calendar. It was only when the Civil Rights marches in 1969 caught the eye of the international media, couched as they were in the context of international civil rights and modelled on the

Black Civil Rights movement in the United States, that the magic circle of the politics of paranoia in Ulster was broken and the longest-surviving paranocracy of modern times began to disintegrate.

Political Immaturity

The resultant fragmentation of Protestant politics in Northern Ireland and the militancy and intransigency of Protestant opinion was inevitable. As Elms (1976) notes 'Studies in areas other than politics . . . suggest that exaggerated trust followed by disillusionment is a reliable recipe for irrational rage.' (p. 7) While the above may seem more appropriate to the description of children's rather than adults' behaviour, it should be kept in mind that the electorate of Northern Ireland is politically immature. Most of the current population has never been involved in a general election where there was ever the remotest possibility of any party other than the Unionist Party forming the next government.

In a parliament of fifty-two representatives, at no general election between 1921 and 1969 did the Unionist/Unofficial Unionist representation total less than thirty-four nor during the same period did the Nationalist/Republican main opposition ever total more than twelve, a zenith last achieved in 1925 (Elliott, 1973). Nor, as argued above, was there ever any other ultimate election issue than the maintenance of the constitutional position. Perhaps most revealing of all, unopposed returns to parliament between 1921 and 1969 averaged 37·5 per cent of the total, reaching a peak of 63·5 per cent in 1933 (average calculated from Elliott, 1973).

Protestant Ulster people had simply no experience of the give and take of normal democratic politics, of the political maturity that comes with experiencing and accepting governments which one may not have voted for, nor of the sobering realisation that the democratic majority does not include oneself. In this respect, local government elections were even worse than general elections. In 1967, for example, only 66 of 496 local governments seats in all the rural districts were contested (Birrell, 1972).

The result has been that many people in Ulster have a concept of government that is grossly oversimplified. Adelson (1971) has shown with young adolescents that twelve and thirteen-year-olds tend to have a highly authoritarian, even bloodthirsty view of government, seeing it in terms of judges and criminals, whereas the typical fifteen-year-old is able to conceive of government as a means for society to function. The fifteen-year-old begins to think of motives other than the criminal's sheer evilness and to consider the long-term as well as the short-term effects of government policies. As a result of Northern Ireland's political petrification, some Ulstermen have a concept of government more appropriate to a twelve- or thirteen-year-old child, in some respects at least, and the prolonged popular feeling that the solution to Ulster's problem lies in law and order measures, understandable as it is, underlines that immaturity.

Just as the Protestant electorate is deficient in its followership capacity through lack of experience, so its leadership has serious deficiencies in its leadership capacity as a consequence of its institutionalised ignorance of the Catholic population. The relationship between Protestant electorate and the Protestant leadership, pathogenic as it was, counterfeit as was the currency of exchange issued by the Unionists, was nonetheless, a transaction. As Homans (1961) notes 'Influence over others is purchased at the price of allowing one's self to be influenced by others.' (p. 286)

Power in Ulster

The relationship between the Protestant leaders of Northern Ireland and the Catholic population was not, until O'Neill began to rock the boat, a matter of transaction or mutual influence, but rather a power relationship of which Rose (1971) comments 'As long as Catholics resided in Northern Ireland, they would be expected to comply with the regime's laws: their support was neither sought nor obtained.' (p. 92)

French and Raven (1959) have put forward the idea that there are five bases for power, namely reward power, coercive power, referent power, expert power and legitimate power. Vis-à-vis the Catholic population in Ulster, the most important have been reward power and coercive power with the latter, in the final analysis, being most important of all.

Reward power over Catholics was basically the better standard of living which Catholics enjoyed as citizens of Northern Ireland as opposed to the Irish Republic. But, as Rose's (1971) survey showed, immediately prior to the present troubles in 1968, 57 per cent of Catholics thought that abolishing the Border would either make no difference or make conditions better economically, as opposed to 24 per cent who thought that conditions would be worsened (there were 19 per cent 'don't knows'). In fact, for both Protestants and Catholics, what they liked most about Northern Ireland were such things as family, friends, countryside, way of life and being where they were born. Good wages and welfare benefits were mentioned by only 9 per cent of Protestants and 11 per cent of Catholics.

Coercive power was based on a gradual scale of might running through electoral majority, the Royal Ulster Constabulary, the now-defunct 'B' Specials (an armed auxiliary police force composed, in practice, entirely of Protestants and perceived by Catholics, with considerable justification, as being anti-Catholic) and finally, the Special Powers Act, traditionally used to intern Catholics indefinitely without trial on suspicion of IRA activities and affording the government a fearsome array of mediaeval, dictatorial powers. Recently a new weapon of coercive power has been added to the armoury in the form of the 'Protestant backlash', the hypothesised (and occasionally realised) unleashing of Protestant violence against Catholics in the face of Catholic intransigence or belligerence. More correctly, this has long been an implicit threat which only recently has been clearly enunciated by Protestant leaders. This weapon has proved to be both lethal and uncontrollable as the scale of Catholic assassinations by Protestant extremists indicates (Dillon and Lehane, 1973). Equally recent and ambivalent as a threat is the increased use of British troops in civilian areas to combat terrorist activities, although local garrison troops were used in the past in much more passive guard roles.

Referent power represents an identification with the source of power such that followers feel that, to some extent at least, the power is being exercised in their best interests, the result being that coercive power no longer has to be used. Terence O'Neill was the first Unionist leader in Northern Ireland to try to exercise this sort of influence (referent power brings us back to the concept of influence rather than power) by his efforts to enlist the support of the Catholic community for the regime. His unprecedented visits to Catholic institutions and organisations, historic meetings with Prime Ministers of the Irish Republic and tentative steps to involve Catholics in the community generally represented his bartering goods.

O'Neill's endeavours did have a considerable influence on Catholic public opinion in Northern Ireland for a time, encouraging, for example, the Nationalist Party, led by Eddie McAteer, to assume the title of Official Opposition in Parliament in 1965, which it had previously resolutely disdained to do. But in 1968, after five years of 'O'Neillism', only 33 per cent of Catholics supported the constitution, while 34 per cent disapproved and 32 per cent didn't know. However, 74 per cent of Catholics believed that there was discrimination against Catholics in Northern Ireland, exactly the same percentage of Protestants believing that there was no such discrimination (Rose, 1971). At least part of the explanation for the Catholics' lack of support for the regime must lie in the fact that discrimination was continuing more or less as normal under O'Neill's administration. Much of it, in any case, was perpetrated by local, rather than central government and by individual employers. In practical terms, O'Neill had not changed much. Psychologically, however, he had raised Catholic expectations of what they might expect from the regime and the gap between expectation and reality was exploited fully by the leaders of the Civil Rights movement in 1969.

There was, therefore, even under O'Neill's government, never any great possibility of Unionist power coming to be seen as legitimate power by the Catholics, based on a mutual acceptance of the aims and ideals of the government by the Unionist leaders and the Catholic community. The final category of power, expert power, arises from valuable specialist knowledge, such as the power exercised by a physician over his patient, and is largely irrelevant in this context.

Terence O'Neill shared many of the prejudices and insensitivities of his Unionist colleagues, despite his urbane veneer and this was starkly revealed in a radio interview a few days after his resignation. He said :

'The basic fear of Protestants in Northern Ireland is that they will be outbred by Roman Catholics. It is as simple as that. It is frightfully hard to explain to a Protestant that if you give

Roman Catholics a good house they will live like Protestants, because they will see their neighbours with cars and television sets.

They will refuse to have eighteen children, but if the Roman Catholic is jobless and lives in a most ghastly hovel, he will rear eighteen children on national assistance.

It is impossible to explain this to a militant Protestant, because he is so keen to deny civil rights to his Roman Catholic neighbours. He cannot understand, in fact, that if you treat Roman Catholics with due consideration and kindness they will live like Protestants, in spite of the authoritative nature of their church'. (*Belfast Telegraph*, 5 May 1969)

However, despite the possession of such sentiments, O'Neill failed to live up to the requirements of a paranocracy. He refused to be paranoid. And no one was more willing or able to point out that inadequacy than Rev Ian Paisley who, in the scope and depth of his endeavours, had developed religio-political paranoia beyond the wildest dreams of his Unionist contemporaries.

Superego-tripping

In the latter half of the 1960s, until events began to overrun them, Unionist leaders were characterised by a debilitating phenomenon which prevented them from dealing realistically with the situation confronting them. They were excessively prone to what Elms (1972) has termed 'superego-tripping', a development of the concept of 'psychism' first identified by Lifton (1968). Elms (1976) notes that superego-tripping is 'acting on the assumption that whatever behaviour best satisfies the demands of one's superego will be most effective in attaining one's realistic goals. In other words, if you judge the effectiveness of your overt acts in terms of whether they make you feel good morally, rather than whether they have changed external reality in the ways you had planned, you're superego-tripping' (p. 50). Superego-tripping, therefore, involves an excess of self-righteousness over common sense.

This term must be distinguished from the recent pop term 'ego-tripping', which is simply self-praise in various forms. Super-ego-tripping, as Elms (1976) points out, is much more dangerous

since the actions which it produces are usually not directed towards self-benefit in any obvious way, but are seen as morally
necessary for the good of all (whether they like it or not).

There is a fine line between superego-tripping and morally
motivated, realistic political endeavour in which concern for the
consequences of one's actions must take precedence over one's
perception of their moral rectitude. This is a difficult area of
interpretation in recent history because it could be argued that
Unionist leaders were concerned with the consequences of their
actions for their Protestant followers. However, in at least some
of the major blunders of leadership, there can be little doubt that
the consequences for the Catholic population, and hence for the
community as a whole, were ignored.

The earliest victim of superego-tripping in the recent situation was William Craig, Minister of Home Affairs in the initial
crisis in 1968. Craig has something of a history of superego-tripping. On one occasion he alienated the entire Trade Union
movement at a time when the O'Neill government was trying
to establish a closer relationship with them by telling them to
'take a running jump'. His moral premise in this case was that
the will of Parliament must not be obstructed (Craig, in Van
Voris, 1975, p. 37). On another occasion in Stormont, he defen-
ded the government against a charge of discriminating against
Catholic lawyers in judicial appointments on the moral premise
that they were educationally and socially inferior and was obliged
to apologise immediately (Devlin, 1975).

It was while William Craig was Minister of Home Affairs
that the first Civil Rights march of the present crisis took place
from Coalisland to Dungannon on 24 August 1968. The issue
was discrimination in local government housing allocation and
the march passed peacefully. The next march was planned for
Londonderry on 5 October and proposed to go through some
traditionally Protestant areas on the grounds that the Civil Rights
group wished to demonstrate itself as being non-sectarian and
willing to include all of the deprived sections of the community,
Protestant and Catholic (Elliot and Hickie, 1971).

This claim was regarded with scepticism and alarm by the
local Protestant community and after various objections, the
Apprentice Boys of Derry, a local Orange group, appeared to
employ an old Ulster tactic by announcing their intention to

celebrate their 'Annual Initiation Ceremony' on the same day and on a route crossing the Civil Rights march. The effect was to warn the police of a potentially dangerous situation to which they were obliged to react by recommending to the Minister of Home Affairs the banning of both marches.

It has almost universally been assumed by commentators of this period, including the Cameron Commission (HMSO, 1969), that the proposed 'annual' event by the Apprentice Boys was entirely bogus. It appears however that there was an annual event around that time of year and that Liverpool Orangemen had made arrangements to travel over to participate on that weekend (*Sunday Times Insight*, 1972). The point, however, was that it was widely viewed as a Protestant counterploy, which to some extent it was since the Apprentice Boys could have chosen a non-conflicting route. Certainly, Craig made no effort to re-route either or both marches to avoid a conflict and simply ordered a ban on marches in Londonderry.

The ban increased support for the march, attracted full media coverage and in the ensuing violence in which the Cameron Report notes that '. . . the police broke ranks and used batons indiscriminately', there were many injuries including Stormont Opposition MPs Gerry Fitt and Eddie McAteer who were batoned 'wholly without justification or excuse' (Cameron). As Elliot and Hickie (1971) comment 'All these events received widespread coverage in the press and violence as a form of behaviour began to be normalised. Various groups were encouraged by these events to organise themselves for further protest.' (p. 53)

This is a perfect example of superego-tripping and the horrors to which it can give rise. Craig's moral premises were (*a*) any Catholic/Republican left wing protest is intrinsically subversive and should be repressed and (*b*) law and order must be seen to be maintained at all costs. The result of his actions was a massive increase in protest and the destruction of respect for the forces of law and order in Ulster. His lack of concern for the consequences of his actions was demonstrated beyond doubt the very next day when a group of students from Queen's University, Belfast, shocked by the events in Londonderry, marched in protest to his home. As Cameron puts it 'Their reception by Mr Craig was hostile and calculated to incense already inflamed feelings.

He so far forgot his position . . . as to call the students generally "silly bloody fools".'

Shortly afterward, on 13 November, Craig announced a one-month ban on all processions within Derry walls to prevent a series of protest marches against police behaviour and the partisan structure of Londonderry Corporation. These were organised by Derry Citizens' Action Committee under the dominant influence of the moderate John Hume. The motive for the marches was partly to defuse the potential violence in Londonderry by doing something active. Craig's ban horrified Prime Minister O'Neill and the then police chief, Inspector-General of the RUC, Sir Albert Kennedy, who resigned immediately on his return from holiday. Of course, three days after Craig's ban, a huge procession of some 15,000 people took place in Londonderry, which the heavy concentration of police simply could not prevent from entering the walls of the inner city. Although little violence took place, the law and its forces were shown to be puny in comparison to the power of the Civil Rights movement.

William Craig's dismissal from the Ministry of Home Affairs on 11 December illustrates another feature of superego-tripping which makes it difficult to prevent, namely that it is not obviously self-interested. Craig must have known that his attitudes and actions could not continue to be tolerated in the O'Neill administration.

Another example of superego-tripping is Terence O'Neill's decisive vote in electing James Chichester-Clark, his cousin, as leader of the Unionist Party on his resignation. Chichester-Clark was a big, amiable and decent man, but totally out of his depth in the political whirlpool he encountered in his period of office from May 1969 to March 1971. The obvious choice for the position in terms of ability, political agility and grass-roots support was Brian Faulkner, O'Neill's long-time adversary and pretender to leadership of the party. O'Neill's superego-trip on this occasion was, at least, honest. He simply said 'Jimmy had only been trying to bring me down for six weeks. Brian had been trying for six years. Childish, isn't it?' (*Sunday Times Insight*, 1972, p. 86).

Unionist leaders, in fact, had been on a continuous superego-trip since the creation of Northern Ireland, although the consequences were a remarkably long time coming. The result was that the habit became so well ingrained that, for many, it was almost a reflex. It was this mode of thinking that led to the initial identification of civil rights demands with extremist Republican plots and to the early and continuing pressure on the British government from some Protestant leaders for a military victory in precedence to a political solution.

Speaking of the early years of the troubles when this line of thought was at its peak, Winchester (1974) describes a typical chain of events :

> 'An arms search provoked a riot; a riot provoked a shooting; a shooting produced an IRA funeral; a funeral produced arrests; the arrests led to court appearances; the court appearances led to riots; the riots led to shooting and the shootings led to deaths. It was, in truth, a vicious circle, and one that no one seemed able even to think about breaking.' (p. 127)

It would not be appropriate to detail every instance of superego-tripping by the Unionist leadership in the train of events subsequent to those described above. The purpose here is merely to define and illustrate a process of Ulster leadership thought, not to chart its every occurrence. It should be noted, however, that the decision which most apparently resembles superego-tripping par excellence in the catastrophic nature of its consequences, namely Brian Faulkner's decision to introduce internment on 9 August 1971, may be just over that fine line between superego-tripping and morally motivated, realistic political endeavour.

Bleakley (1974) argues that Faulkner's attitude to internment was set by his period as Minister of Home Affairs from 1959 to 1963 during which internment was in operation and during which the IRA campaign of the 1950s came to an end. Faulkner appears to have been convinced of its efficacy in ending that campaign although he seemed to regard it as a last resort and had consistently voted against internment in Chichester-Clark's cabinet (Winchester, 1974). Nor from the ranks of the police, the army or the British Cabinet was any rational alternative put forward whose effects could predictably achieve the same or better ends than those expected of internment (*Sunday Times Insight*, 1972). Hence the introduction of internment by Faulkner does not fall within the specifications of superego-tripping. It should, therefore, be clear that the concept of superego-tripping must be applied with considerable caution in such political analyses.

Rev Ian Paisley

Of the major Protestant leaders who crossed the stage of Northern Irish politics in the 1960s and early 1970s, only Rev Ian Paisley remains a major force. Terence O'Neill has long since left the province, James Chichester-Clark has retired from the political arena, Brian Faulkner is dead and William Craig lost his Westminster seat in the British general election of May 1979, although it is unlikely that this defeat represents his last political gasp. In that Ian Paisley is a political leader of considerable durability, it may be instructive to examine his career as a specific example of leadership in Northern Ireland.

If the Unionist Party had sown the slow-flowering seeds of its own destruction over the half-century prior to its present demise, and if the events of 1969 provided the water for their growth, then it can be said that the Rev Ian Paisley, almost single-handedly, provided the heat (some might say the manure) that accelerated that growth. By far the most complex character ever to cross the political scene in Ulster, Paisley has infuriated, perplexed, confused, amused, and fascinated his observers. He is, in fact, the embodiment of much of Ulster's complexities and what one Belfastman once said of Ulster is also true of him : 'Anyone who isn't confused here doesn't really understand what is going on'.

However, despite the complexities of the man, the task of understanding him is a labour of necessity and Bowyer Bell has spelt out the reasons why this is so. First, he notes that 'Unlike Edward Carson, James Craig or Basil Brooke, Paisley is of the people in whose name he speaks, which is one reason he will be there at the end, whenever that is'. Second, he comments that '. . . Ian Paisley is the best introduction to what the consciousness of large sections of the Protestant poor is all about'.

Ian Paisley was born in Armagh in 1926 and his father was from a poor North Tyrone mountain family (Harris, 1972 gives an excellent account of life in such a community in Ulster). His father was a Baptist preacher who eventually formed his own small church and family discipline was strict. Marrinan (1973), relates that Ian Paisley was not allowed to go with his school class to see the film 'David Copperfield' since, in his father's view, cinemas were satanic emporia. Despite his bitter disappointment, Ian obeyed his father. But beneath the exterior, his father appears to have been kind and soft-hearted and Ian Paisley was genuinely close to him.

At sixteen, he went to the Barrie School of Evangelism in Wales, 'renowned for its piety rather than its learning' (Boulton, 1973) and, a year later, he switched to the Theological Hall of the Reformed Presbyterian Church, Belfast. He emerged from this institution in 1945 'highly recommended as a student and preacher of the Gospel.'

Paisley launched himself on a career as a gospel preacher, based in the Ravenhill Evangelical Mission near the shipyard in East Belfast but preaching throughout the province. Almost from the beginning of his career, he linked religious evangelism to politics in Northern Ireland and beyond. Abbott (1973) has argued that Paisley's particular form of political evangelism places him in the tradition of right-wing fundamentalists in the United States. Certainly, his links with and tours in the 'Bible Belt' in the United States and his flair for media utilisation and fund-raising show that he is aware of and has learned from that tradition. But Scott's (1976) analysis, placing him in the particularly Ulster line of Protestant political evangelists, after the style of Henry Cooke, Thomas Drew and Hugh Hanna, is undoubtedly more valid.

A consistent motivational conflict is apparent in Paisley's career. He is very aware of his own abilities, which are considerable and to which almost no serious commentator of the Ulster scene has failed to give credit, even if somewhat grudgingly. At the same time, while wishing to see these abilities appropriately recognised, he has often lacked the confidence to put them to a proper test.

An example of this conflict of ambition and self-doubt is his history of educational and intellectual qualifications. In 1954 he acquired by post a B.D., and an honorary D.D., from the Pioneer Theological Seminary at Rockford, Illinois, officially listed by the United States Department of Higher Education as a 'bogus degree mill'. In 1958, he obtained by post an M.A., from Burton College and Seminary at Manitou Springs, Colorado, another bogus degree mill. (Marrinan, 1973). On top of all this, he paid a subscription to the Royal Geographical Society which entitled him to put F.R.G.S. after his name, became a member of the 'Royal Society of Literature' (M.R.S.L.) and a Fellow of the 'Philosophical Society of Great Britain' (F.P.L.S.) (Boulton, 1973).

All of these dubious distinctions were dropped in 1966 when, after his release from prison, he was awarded an honorary doctorate of divinity by the Bob Jones University of Greenville, Carolina. This institution, a cut above his former alma maters, still lacks any official accreditation as an educational establishment. It is, in fact, an all-white, well-funded, bible college, with puritanical rules of social conduct for its students, and has previously honoured such luminaries as George Wallace and Barry Goldwater.

Although, in the latter case, Dr Paisley was a passive recipient rather than an active seeker of his academic title, there is really no reason why he could not have achieved a proper academic distinction in theology. First, he is a very intelligent man with an unerring nose for illogicality, in others at least. Many a poor commentator or politician, coming forward with self-righteous but woolly indignation to protest a point with Paisley, has seen a superficially good case dismembered, limb by logical limb, with withering scorn and skill. He frequently achieves this effect by choosing limited premises, but unwary opponents who fail to respond accordingly or imagine that their argument is sufficiently robust to withstand the alteration in its intended application, are made to look foolish.

Second, despite the much-published and hair-raising fulminations on this and that, most particularly the Roman Catholic Church and ecumenism, there is evidence that a reflective Paisley is capable of relatively profound theological insights. Marrinan (1973), whose biography of Paisley is as sympathetic as one would expect of an upper class, devoutly Catholic ex-London barrister living in Dublin, has commented that Paisley's treatise on the Epistles of St Paul, written while serving a prison sentence in the Crumlin Road Prison, is of considerable theological value, despite the circumstances under which it was written.

Third, the man's computer-like capacity for scriptural reference plus his strength of application would be enormously helpful in the study of theology. And finally, in practical terms, even critical observers of his preaching and ministration in his church in Belfast have commented very favourably on his pastoral performance (Dudley Edwards, 1970; Cruise O'Brien, 1972).

There have been occasions, however, in which Paisley's self-confidence about his ability has brought him under close academic scrutiny and he has survived remarkably well. On one notable occasion, he undertook what for most people would be the daunting task of proposing the motion 'That the Roman Catholic Church has no place in the twentieth century' at Oxford University. The date was 23 November 1967 and the debate was televised. At this time, Paisley was at the height of his notoriety, the demon of the liberal left, myself included, and was no doubt invited partly for the fun of watching a lunatic preacher from Ulster make a public fool of himself. It is almost certain that Paisley was only too well aware of this motive and his acceptance, therefore, underlines his self-confidence and his need to have his ability recognised.

Marrinan (1973) recalls the debate as an affront to decency, dwelling on one particular incident, certainly in questionable taste, in which Paisley held aloft a holy wafer and questioned the theological validity of regarding it as representing the body of Christ, as Catholics do. The speaker against the motion was Norman St John Stevas, MP, a prominent member of the British Conservative Party, a leading Roman Catholic layman and a somewhat mannered and supercilious individual.

A number of things emerged in the debate. First, the lunatic preacher from Ulster was not intimidated by the distinction of his surroundings, the critical reputation of his audience or the position of his opponent. Second, he could present a reasoned case with clarity, skill and humour as well as conviction. Third, he could maintain his integrity and dignity even under these difficult, strange and testing circumstances. I recall watching the debate on television and feeling a curious sort of pride, which I believe was reasonably general among contemporary Belfast students at the time, that even an Ulster lunatic was not to be taken lightly, by Oxford University, Norman St John Stevas or anyone else.

Apart from academic distinction, Paisley has tended to take short cuts in other spheres to establish himself, although as we shall see, this case can be overargued. On leaving college in 1945, he founded a National Union of Protestants with himself at the head and started a paper, *The Protestant* with himself as editor (Boulton, 1973). The paper lasted only for a few issues but it was an astonishingly ambitious move for a nineteen-year-old working class young man in 1945 Belfast.

Ian Paisley's clerical career also demonstrates an ambitious impatience with, and perhaps fear of, conventional clerical progress and its limitations. He was ordained by his father in his church when he was twenty-one. After a series of gospel campaigns in which he inveighed against the theological liberalism of the Presbyterian Church, some congregational splits began to occur with breakaway 'Free Presbyterian Churches' being formed. Paisley organised these churches into the Free Presbyterian Church of Ulster with himself as Moderator. He was twenty-five years old at this time and his church subsequently flourished. Its success is symbolised by his new £200,000 church in the Ravenhill Road, Belfast, one of the most expensive new churches built anywhere in the United Kingdom since World War II and the jewel in his string of twenty odd churches in Northern Ireland and the Republic.

Superficially, his career in politics can be seen in a similar light to other aspects of his career. In 1966, he formed the Ulster Constitution Defence Committee with himself as chairman. This was his first overtly political vehicle. Subsequently he founded the Protestant Unionist Party which later became the Democratic Unionist Party, with himself as leader. Some commentators argue the 'short-cut' theory even further, claiming that Paisley deliberately surrounds himself with talentless colleagues to promote his personal domination of the movement. On closer examination, however, it becomes clear that Paisley's political career has been uncharacteristically cautious and his personal role somewhat circumscribed.

In retrospect, Paisley has been extremely slow to make an explicitly political move, despite his early intermingling of politics and religion. Boulton (1973) records that in the late 1940s he had begun to appear on Unionist Party platforms and that on 12 July 1949, he shared a platform with the recently-elected Brian Faulkner. Marrinan (1973) claims that in this period he took elocution lessons and that he practised public speaking in council election campaigns in the early 1950s. Marrinan also notes that he was not liked by the ruling Unionists, no doubt partly because of his lowly background, and that he curried no favours from them. Possibly he was overawed by the might of the Unionist Party machine and, almost certainly, he did not forget his rejection. He did not, at any rate, rush headlong into the quest for personal political office and apart from a brief flirtation with the idea of standing for election in East Belfast in 1959, he did not stand as a candidate until he opposed Terence O'Neill ten years later in the Bannside constituency.

In fact, rather than pushing himself forward into political activity, Paisley seemed to be content to back others who were standing for policies broadly similar to his own. For example, he supported Desmond Boal's candidacy in the 1960 by-election because he was 'a man who put protestantism first—not like those who became Protestants and Orangemen when they are looking for nomination' (*Nusight*, October 1969, p. 12). Also, in the 1964 Belfast Corporation elections, he fielded four Protestant Unionist candidates, including his wife.

When Paisley was eventually elected to the Westminster Parliament in June 1970 (he was already at this time a Stormont MP), he maintained a very low profile for several months. At the end of this period he emerged as a widely-acknowledged, effective parliamentarian with a sound knowledge of the system and procedures of Westminster. All of those things tend to suggest that Paisley's approach to politics has been careful, reflective and cautious. Unfortunately, the truth of this point is lost in the media coverage of Paisley's latest involvement in some rowdy and destructive piece of political protest, for it is to protest that he most naturally gravitates and it is in protest that he makes best television fodder and worst political leader. Moreover, such incidents confirm his popular international image as the mad Irish preacher.

The charge that Paisley has tended to surround himself with inferiors in order that he may dominate is based on equally suspect premises. It is certainly true that some of his closest colleagues seem limited in vision and ability, but the premise on which the charge is based assumes that Ulster Protestant politics is filled with men of sparkling ability and that Paisley's brand of politics attracts at least a proportional share of such talent whom Paisley avoids lest he may, by comparison, shine less brightly. This is probably untrue. Moreover, his closest mentor and a man who has clearly influenced his political outlook on several impor-

tant issues, is Desmond Boal, Q.C. Boal is a man of very considerable influence and ability and was joint-founder with Paisley
of the Democratic Unionist Party. Dillon and Lehane (1973)
describe him thus: 'He was considered the party's most powerful political thinker. He was also the most brilliant barrister in
Northern Ireland, and probably in the whole of the United
Kingdom.' (p. 135) He, at least, is scarcely the stuff of which dull
colleagues are made.

Paisley is what Weber (1921) has described as a 'charismatic
leader', that is one whose personal qualities attract followers.
One source of attraction is that such leaders express publicly
what followers had been feeling privately, but perhaps only
vaguely. In the context of O'Neill's premiership in Ulster and his
moves towards a rapprochement with the traditional enemies of
the Ulster Protestant, the usual outpourings of anti-Catholic
sentiments from time to time had been discouraged. Thus
Paisley's anti-ecumenical, anti-Republican speeches were welcomed by a somewhat stifled and confused portion of the Ulster
Protestant electorate. Gerry Fitt, the former leader of the Social
Democratic and Labour Party, commented at the time that 'the
biggest crime that Paisley has committed, the cardinal sin which
he has committed, is saying in public what a lot of Unionists
think in private' (*Nusight*, 1969, p. 14-15).

Paisley, like other charismatic leaders such as John F. Kennedy
and Martin Luther King (charisma is ecumenical), developed a
talent for aphorism, succinctly summarising and mobilising
Protestant feeling in apt language. Although his language was
often archaic and, to the outside world, the sentiments laughable
(Scott, 1976), Paisley's rhetorical outpourings were vitally appropriate to his followers. Hollander (1976) emphasises this rela-
tional process in charisma which means that others must perceive
charisma for it to exist, although for some it may have no appeal
at all. On ecumenical matters, for instance, Paisley bemoaned
after a visit to the pope by the Anglican Prelate that 'the Archbishop of Canterbury had gone to swim in the unholy waters of
Rome'. Or, of O'Neill's meetings with Prime Ministers of the
Irish Republic, he lamented O'Neill's 'shaking hands with men
who were covered in the blood of Britons' (*Nusight*, 1969, p. 12).

Much has been written and broadcast about the excesses of Ian
Paisley and his followers in the 1960s and it is certainly true that

E

Paisley's attacks on the Roman Catholic Church, ecumenism and 'O'Neillism' were not objectively reasonable, although reason is a somewhat wispy weapon to wield against religious and political philosophies or their antitheses. What is beyond doubt is that Paisley's efforts contributed in no small degree to the deterioration of inter-community feeling in Ulster and to the promotion of violence on several well-documented occasions. It is Paisley's single greatest weakness that he fails to perceive the effect of his rhetoric on minds less subtle and less morally principled than his own. For while Paisley has preached anti-ecumenism, anti-Republicanism and anti-Catholicism, his supporters have often acted simply against individual Catholics per se.

For example, it appears that at least one of the three UVF men charged with the Malvern Street murder in 1966, in which one Catholic was shot dead and two others seriously wounded, was misled by the message of (early) Paisleyism into his involvement in the crime. He allegedly said to the police on his arrest 'I am terribly sorry I ever heard tell of that man Paisley or decided to follow him. I am definitely ashamed of myself to be in such a position.' Although Paisley instantly condemned the crime publicly 'the UVF was largely a product of his own rhetoric and some of his closest associates were UVF men' (Boulton, 1973, p. 51).

Despite the mud (or blood) which justifiably stuck to Paisley on this and less dramatically on other occasions, it is unlikely that such deeds are consistent with his personality or philosophy. Like his father, Ian Paisley is a personally warm and kind man behind the façade and not just, as the public image would suggest, to Protestants. Bernadette Devlin visited him at his home in October 1968 and was surprised by his warmth and the clamorous normality of his family life (*Sunday Times Insight*, 1972). But this is typical of the paradoxical nature of inter-group relations in Northern Ireland.

The paradox lies in the proclamation of institutional and collective insults by each community about the other while at the same time extending personal and individual kindness where appropriate. Rosemary Harris (1972) has vividly depicted this schizoid relationship in Ulster, although in times of inter-communal conflict, the relationship tends to break down into a more psychologically consistent, if less desirable one. When

Bernadette Devlin, then unmarried, announced that she was pregnant in July 1971, Paisley's comment about a bitter opponent, amid the jackal din of political glee, proclaimed his personal philosophy: 'I have no comment to make whatsoever. All I can quote is what Lord Jesus Christ said "He that has no sin, let him cast the first stone".' (*Target*, 1975, p. 329)

Indeed, Paisley's philosophy, although clearly open to misinterpretation at times, is quite explicit in its promulgation of the personal worth of others. In the 1950s, Paisley directed much of his energy towards converting Catholics to Protestantism, including one notorious case in 1956 in which he refused to divulge the whereabouts of a missing fifteen-year-old Catholic girl 'convert', Maura Lyons, to prevent her falling back into the influence of the Catholic Church (Marrinan, 1973). In other words, Paisley's target was not the individual Catholic, who was worthy of being brought into the fold, but Catholicism itself. And when Paisley attacks individuals, such as the Pope, Terence O'Neill and so forth, they are attacked as leading proponents of particular philosophies, even though his rhetorical surge often brings personal abuse in its wake. Of Bernadette Devlin, for instance, he said 'The murder in this young woman's heart boils to the surface and spills from her mouth as she screams . . . (Her) veins are polluted with the venom of popish tuition. . . .' (*Target*, 1975, p. 18). The subtlety of that implicit distinction between the person as a figurehead and the person as an individual is lost on many of his followers.

Dudley Edwards (1970), writing of a visit to Paisley's church in Belfast and recounting the sermon, notes Paisley's dwelling on the topics of mutual respect between Protestants and Catholics and loving one's neighbour. On this occasion he emphasised the necessity of carrying out this principle into practice with Catholic neighbours. Dudley Edwards comments 'I found myself wondering how many ministers and priests—of any religion—had said anything remotely like this in Northern Ireland that Sunday' (p. 13). In addition, Paisley has an excellent constituency record as an MP with both Catholics and Protestants (Bowyer Bell, 1976).

Ian Paisley is one of those people with whom journalists (and psychologists) are least happy in dealing with because he defies simplistic analysis. David McKittrick, a seasoned commentator on Ulster, declared in the *Irish Times* in November 1977 that 'There is one central fact to be remembered about the Big Man— that he does not change.' Unfortunately, one imagines that this comment had more to do with exasperation than considered judgment, for nothing could be further from the truth. There has been a long line of contradictory and, with hindsight, often foolish judgments about Paisley in the press. In 1966, the *Irish Independent* was finding him laughable and Martin Wallace of the *Belfast Telegraph* had concluded that 'he is not to be taken seriously as a political force'. However, misperceptions of Paisley may have their basis in social science rather than journalism, as we shall see below.

One of the most influential social psychological works of this century, *The Authoritarian Personality* (Adorno et al., 1950), puts forward the view that authoritarians have a consistency of personality which is evident in a wide variety of uniformly right-wing and bigoted views about social issues, and that the genesis of this syndrome lies in a childhood in which sexual and aggressive impulses are harshly handled by authoritarian parents. The result is a person who grows up with an inability to cope with and fear of his own impulses which tend to be externalised or projected onto outgroups (often minorities), an over-developed and petrifying view of his own station in life and the appropriate station of others, and an over-idealised view of authority and authority figures.

Such people are popularly referred to as bigots, although it is open to question whether bigotry and authoritarianism are psychologically identical. In any case, the educated layman is aware of the results of this research, although he may never have heard of its authors (Elms, 1976), and holds the (often disparagingly expressed) view that bigots are inflexible, ultra-conservative individuals who have the greatest difficulty in altering their attitudes and beliefs because of their deep-seated origins.

In this context, therefore, it is obvious why Paisley was so easily miscatalogued. He was a bellowing demagogue with an unseemly following of bigoted working class Protestants, shouting aloft religious and political sentiments more appropriate to the seventeenth than to the twentieth century. He held emotion-raising public meetings whose form and style smacked of fascism. He hastened Captain O'Neill's exit from office just when he was beginning to drag Ulster from the past and so forth. He was, in short, 'Ulster Protestant man in all his ugly reality' as the *New Statesman* described him—a bigot par excellence and bigots are, of course, inflexible, ultra-conservative etc.

In fact, however, the research conducted by Adorno and his colleagues, which addressed itself primarily to anti-semitism, has been subject to a considerable degree of valid criticism by subsequent researchers, most particularly in regard to doubts about the methods by which the original data was obtained (cf. Brown, 1965). A much less neat and simple picture of authoritarianism has been emerging in recent years. Concepts such as dogmatism (Rokeach, 1954; Rokeach, 1960), conservatism (McCloskey, 1958, Wilson, 1973), socio-economic conservatism and tough-mindedness (Eysenck, 1975), all partial substitutes for, or facets of, authoritarianism, have complicated matters. Bigotry per se is a little researched concept and it is not at all clear where it fits into this disintegrating picture. All of these subsequent complications, in any case, overlook the fact that Adorno and his associates never claimed that everyone who held authoritarian views conformed to their theoretically neat syndrome, which became 'common knowledge', but only that there was a tendency for such a package of present views and past upbringing to occur in their sample of subjects.

Be that as it may, Paisley's actions tend to have been interpreted in the light of the simplified version of 'the facts' about authoritarians or bigots. The result has been that where those actions deviated from the image, they were seen as not genuinely motivated, or they were somewhat awkwardly noted in surprise and then forgotten so that subsequent statements of the 'Big Man never changes' type could be made to restore order to confused perceptions. Such a process is a perfectly normal facet of our cognitive processes and this tendency toward cognitive consistency has been explored by a number of psychologists, most prominently Festinger (1957). An example of the wry incredulity with which some of Paisley's image-inconsistent actions have been greeted is the reported comment of one of the SDLP leaders subsequent to Paisley's meeting with them. He commented 'Wolfe Tone is alive and well and leading the Democratic Unionist Party' (Boulton, 1973).

However, Paisley fits the mould of bigot only superficially.

Certainly, his philosophy is, in some respects, old-fashioned and his opposition to Catholicism fervent. And if ecumenism is a left-ward trend, then he is on the far right. Equally, in political terms, if power-sharing is a moderate or even leftish policy, then again he is on the far right.

In contrast to this, many of Paisley's political attitudes are well to the left in the context of Ulster politics. Desmond Boal has described the DUP as 'right wing in the sense of being strong on the constitution and restoring security, but to the left on social policies'. As mentioned above, Paisley has met secretly with the largely Catholic-supported SDLP and found a wide basis of agreement on social policy (Boulton, 1973). Significantly, he has eschewed any links between his party and the Orange Order (of which he is not a member) on the grounds that such links are undemocratic. Indeed Boal has gone so far as to attack the traditional Unionist link with the Orange Order as being as bad as the Roman Catholic Church's influence on Southern Irish politics.

Along with the SDLP, Paisley opposed the introduction of internment 'in principle' (although he had initially favoured it) and such is the resistance to the notion that he can actually change, that this is almost universally attributed to his supposed realisation that internment would be used against loyalists. It seems just as likely that his association with Desmond Boal Q.C. had resulted in a heightened awareness of the ultimate folly of judicial inequity and that he did finally object 'in principle'. This is, at least, consistent with his lone and unsuccessful opposition to the introduction of a previous inequitable law, the Criminal Justice (Temporary Provisions) (Northern Ireland) Act of 1970, described by Winchester (1974) as 'an appalling piece of legis-lation' (p. 64). Winchester comments that 'Only Ian Paisley, to his everlasting credit, fought the Bill in Parliament as being too ambiguous and too imprecise.' (p. 65)

On the abolition of Stormont and the introduction of direct rule from Westminster, only Paisley, of all the Protestant politi-cians, emerged from the situation with any credibility. His sources at Westminster were obviously better than anyone else's since he announced on 30 October 1971 that direct rule was imminent (it was introduced on 24 March 1972) and welcomed it as a means of integrating Northern Ireland more closely with the United Kingdom. This contrasted with Brian Faulkner's ridicule of the suggestion and threats of a 'violent holocaust' should it happen and with William Craig's empty howls of a Vanguard (an erstwhile militant Protestant 'umbrella' organisation) uprising and declaration of independence for Northern Ireland should Stormont be abolished.

All in all, it does seem quite clear that Paisley has been prepared to change and to risk his reputation with his followers by departing radically from traditional Unionist stances on major issues. Indeed he has gone too far too fast at times, such as his comments on radio in the Republic of Ireland and in the *Irish Times* in which he stated that if Protestants could be sure that the Catholic Church could no longer dictate policy to the Dublin government, and the theocratic nature of the 1937 Constitution were altered, 'then there would be a new set of circumstances, where there could be neighbourliness in the highest possible sense, and in those circumstances there would be a situation different from any that existed when the country was divided.'

The reaction to these ideas in the Republic was overwhelming with acclamation from a number of sources. The loyalist reaction, however, was puzzlement and dismay. Paisley realised that he had gone too far and immediately began to claim that he had been misreported, misquoted and misunderstood. He reverted to the more familiar sounds of 'no surrender' and resistance to popish encroachment, but the incident cost him support to other Protestant leaders, such as William Craig.

In this regard, it is instructive to examine Paisley's political career in the context of Hollander's (1958; 1964) research into the processes by which leaders can initiate changes in group goals or group orientation. Hollander argues that a leader must build up a 'credit balance' of 'idiosyncrasy credits' by conforming to group expectations and by being perceived as competent in his leadership. This perceived conformity and competence results in a subsequent tolerance (but not an indefinite tolerance) of the leader's pursuit of new goals for the group or of radical methods of obtaining old goals. Within the context of this model of leadership, Paisley's apparent vacillation between traditional and radical stances begins to make sense.

Clearly then the Rev Ian Paisley is a great deal more flexible and positive as a leader than he is customarily given credit for.

It seems, if this analysis is correct, that his appreciation of the necessary give and take relationship between leader and followers has required him to adopt generally unhelpful or even destructive stances at times in order that he may not alienate an already confused and disillusioned Protestant followership. For while the electorate of Ulster is politically immature, recent years have unleashed upon them a deluge of political changes which would strain the comprehension of sophisticated political savants anywhere, were changes of similar scope introduced to their political world. The labyrinth of political fact and fantasy which sustained them for half a century has been swept away overnight to be replaced by the administrative holding operation of direct rule.

It is possible to view, for example, Paisley's wrecking of the Constitutional Convention in August 1975 and his unsuccessful attempt to generate a second all-out loyalist strike in May 1977 as examples of his sensitivity to grass roots pressure. The fact that he appears to have misjudged that pressure on the latter occasion is beside the point, although it is perhaps worth mentioning that there are suggestions from reliable sources within Northern Ireland, that the media deliberately misrepresented the level of support for the strike in order to curtail its effectiveness.

The intention of this analysis of leadership in Ulster has been to examine the nuts and bolts of the relationship between leaders and followers in Northern Ireland. It has been argued that while that relationship had a certain psychological validity under the exclusively Protestant leadership which traditional Unionism offered, O'Neill's attempts to lead the entire community ultimately led to a perceived breach of the transaction between Unionist leadership and Protestant electorate, which they were not prepared to countenance. Subsequent events, symbolised by the abolition of the Stormont government, revealed the counterfeit currency with which Unionists had been bartering and resulted in a disillusioned and angry fragmentation of Ulster Protestant politics.

In this context, the achievement of Ian Paisley in maintaining the loyalty of a large group of Protestant followers and in influencing many more, while pursuing policies and suggesting directions occasionally radical in the Ulster context, is remarkable, although, for a variety of reasons, his image is a great deal worse than his actual record. Good or bad, however, and there will be many who strongly disagree with the interpretation put forward here, Paisley and his followers will, as Bowyer Bell has observed, be there at the end, whenever it is as his triumph in the recent European Election indicates. And at that point, it will have been worthwhile to consider the man and his followers in a different, if unfamiliar perspective.

CHAPTER SIX

Growing up in Northern Ireland

In looking at the children and young people of Northern Ireland, this chapter will, inevitably, be concerned with the future of the province. I will try to examine, by reviewing relevant research, the attitudes and likely future behaviour of Northern Irish children and look ahead towards possible developments which could, and I believe would, result in significant and beneficial changes in inter-group relations in the province. First, however, it may be instructive to examine some of the 'bread and butter' problems facing young people in Northern Ireland.

The July 1978 figures for unemployment in Northern Ireland showed that 13·4 per cent of the workforce was unemployed, compared to 6·6 per cent in the rest of the United Kingdom. This was the highest figure since 1938, yet it conceals unemployment rates of hair-raising proportions in certain areas of Ulster and in certain areas of the city of Belfast, as studies by the Queen's University Department of Geography and others indicate (Boal, Doherty and Pringle, 1974). Within this context, the prospects for young school-leavers seeking employment are bleak, especially for those without formal qualifications.

Compounding the problem of unemployment is the fact that wages in the province are on average only 86 per cent of wages in Great Britain based on 1974 data (*Regional Statistics*, No 11, 1975) and the province has proportionately twice as many people as Great Britain on very low pay, again based on 1974 figures and using £30 per week as the standard. To gild the economic lily, prices, apart from housing, are generally higher in Northern Ireland than elsewhere in the United Kingdom and even the cost of housing has increased sharply towards the United Kingdom level in recent years.

The combination of these circumstances, plus the fact that

Northern Irish families tend to be larger than families in Great Britain, has led to the situation that while Northern Ireland contains only 2·8 per cent of the total United Kingdom population, it receives 11·4 per cent of all payments made to supplement the earnings of low-income families where the head of the household is in full-time employment. Eileen Evason, in her 1976 booklet entitled *Poverty: the facts in Northern Ireland*, points out that while family size is a more important factor in producing reliance on Family Income Supplement in Northern Ireland than Great Britain, low wages are a more important factor than large families in Northern Ireland. This judgment hinges on precisely what definition of 'large family' one chooses to make, but 30 per cent of Northern Irish claimants have two or less children, 47 per cent three or less children, and 65 per cent four or less children. Evason (1976) estimates that, in all, nearly 200,000 children under sixteen in Northern Ireland, that is to say almost 40 per cent of all children, are being brought up in families with resources below the official needs level.

What sort of housing do Northern Ireland's children have to grow up in? In 1970, Evason notes, 33 per cent of dwellings in the province had been built before 1881, 15 per cent had been erected between 1921 and 1941, and 40 per cent were built in the post-war period, many of the latter being worst of all from the point of view of public amenities, community development and standard of design and construction.

The Housing Condition Survey conducted by the Northern Ireland Housing Executive in 1974 found that 19·6 per cent of the housing stock in the province (almost 90,000 dwellings) were unfit for habitation; the comparable 1971 British figure was 7·3 per cent. In all, 38 per cent of dwellings were either unfit, lacked basic amenities such as internal w.c. or a fixed bath, or required repairs costing (at that time) £250 or more. In comparison to United Kingdom standards, Northern Irish dwellings are grossly lacking in basic amenities. According to the 1975 Northern Ireland Housing Survey, published by the Northern Ireland Housing Executive in 1976, 17·2 per cent of Northern Irish households occupy dwellings with an insufficient number of bedrooms, a burden borne mainly by manual workers, with larger families inevitably worst affected.

In regard to the latter problem, the situation cannot be relieved by sending young children to nursery education, because there is very little provision for it. Northern Ireland has roughly one place for every seventy-five children compared to one place for every thirteen children in England and Wales.

A concomitant of all these hardships, and especially the housing situation, is that the standard of health in Northern Ireland is lower than in other United Kingdom regions, despite the fact that the Health Service, in terms of staffing and provision, compares very favourably with other parts of the United Kingdom. The infant mortality rate at twenty-one per thousand live births is 24 per cent higher than the United Kingdom figure on 1974 figures and these overall statistics disguise alarming rates of infant mortality in specific areas, particularly in the West. Omagh, for example, has recorded rates of infant mortality of the order of thirty to thirty-five per thousand live births.

These statistics represent the background against which the problems of growing up in Northern Ireland must be seen. As with all such statistics, they have a tendency to deaden the reality which they represent and to bear less repetition than more dramatic and tangible, though inevitably less representative, glimpses of the difficulties which young people in Ulster face. The summary of these figures is, however, simple enough. A large percentage of Northern Irish children are growing up in inadequate housing, in poor economic circumstances, facing the prospect of prolonged unemployment and possibly ill-health. But it is to the more dramatic aspects of life in Northern Ireland which we now turn.

Perhaps the most widely received, certainly the most vigorously disseminated accounts of stress on Northern Ireland's children have been given by local psychiatrists, Fraser and Lyons. These authors have published a plethora of studies (Fraser, 1971a, 1971b, 1972, 1974; Lyons, 1971a, 1971b, 1972a, 1972b, 1972c, 1973a, 1973b, 1973c, 1974a, 1974b, 1975) many of them frankly repetitive and methodically limited. In Chapter Three the methodological and theoretical approach of several studies by these authors was critically appraised in regard to their work with adults in troubled areas and most of these criticisms would also apply in this context. In this chapter, the intention is to give a reasonably global account of the difficulties and prospects of

Northern Irish children and so their work must be judged according to its contribution to that task.

Both Fraser and Lyons concentrated their attention on the more dramatic aspects of the situation in the early years of the conflict, looking at the inhabitants of the most troubled areas. Their focus was on the sorts of psychological effects which exposure to rioting, shooting and bombing occasioned. In the main, both authors commented upon the general resilience of Northern Ireland's youngsters and the observed nightmares, enuresis and phobias appeared to be generally short-lived. This is consistent with the findings on disturbances among children as a result of air raids on Britain during the Second World War, where the stress of evacuation separation was found to be more disturbing than the effects of the raids themselves (Bodman, 1941; Burbury 1941; Mons, 1941; Bowlby, 1952). In many cases, the phobias were adaptive in the sense that they removed the children from anxiety-provoking situations and afforded them an opportunity to express their anxiety.

As one might expect, the evidence suggested that it was children, who were in some way vulnerable, who were most likely to suffer symptoms severe enough to require medical attention (Fraser, 1971a), which was also the gist of the findings with adults (Lyons, 1973a, 1973b). In particular, having one or both parents themselves emotionally disturbed by the violence, was an especially potent precipitating factor. The particular type of symptom, according to Fraser (1971a), seemed related to the child's personality strengths and weaknesses. For example, shy and timid children might develop double vision, preventing them from going out on the street.

The data which Fraser and Lyons presented bore largely on the transient symptoms of disturbance among vulnerable children in riot-torn areas of the province, primarily in Belfast. On this basis, they speculated on the long-term effects on children of being conditioned to violence and having violence rewarded in troubled times by peers and, indeed, adults. As Lyons (1973b) put it '. . . one might anticipate that when peace returns to Northern Ireland there will be a continuing epidemic of violent and anti-social behaviour amongst teenagers' (p. 167). I will return to this question later.

There is a growing body of literature, however, which has

addressed itself to more representative, less transient aspects of the life of children in Northern Ireland and it is this work to which we now turn our attention.

Ungoed-Thomas (1972) sought to illuminate patterns of relationships and behaviour among Northern Irish adolescents, using a critical incident technique. In this method, subjects are asked to describe a situation which illustrates a theme of interest to the investigator. For example, one of the questions asked of adolescents was 'Describe a situation in which someone treated you badly or made you feel angry'. The subjects were 1,257 Protestant and Catholic adolescents mainly from Belfast and Londonderry, but included some rural adolescents. The distribution of responses by theme showed that, apart from the expected preoccupation with violence (the study was carried out in 1970-1971), Northern Irish adolescents were unusually concerned about social difficulties with strangers and preoccupied with their families. This contrasts with the more typical preoccupation of British adolescents with boy/girl relationships (McPhail, Ungoed-Thomas and Chapman, 1972).

This finding is consistent with the contention of Spencer (1974), based on admittedly impressionistic evidence, that a major influence on the strength of the present conflict has been that the process of urbanisation (the psychological as opposed to physical process), with its attendant sophistication and social tolerance, has been retarded, if not entirely stunted in both parts of Ireland. It would appear from Ungoed-Thomas's findings that Northern Irish adolescents do have a more traditional, rural outlook than their counterparts in Great Britain.

Ungoed-Thomas found in his study a preoccupation with violence among adolescents in Ulster at that time. Other researchers have noted a ready facility with the paraphernalia of conflict among children both in troubled areas (Jahoda and Harrison, 1975) and in trouble-free areas (Cairns, Hunter and Herring, 1978). Russell (1973), in a major survey of some 3,000 Ulster schoolboys throughout the province, found that 50 to 60 per cent of primary schoolboys and 60 to 70 per cent of secondary schoolboys thought it acceptable to use violence for political ends. However, in Russell's data, there was evidence of ambivalence towards the situation, with 40 per cent of secondary schoolboys and 33 per cent of primary schoolboys already thinking of leaving the province when they were older. In addition, those who believed most strongly in political violence were not necessarily those who approved of general vandalism.

However, leaving aside for the moment the implications of these findings for the question of actual or potential anti-social behaviour among Northern Irish youth, we might ask how and why this preoccupation with violence and conflict-related phenomena arises. An outside observer might well reply that these questions are naïve in a small geographical area which has seen violence and conflict on the scale enacted in Northern Ireland during the last decade. And indeed, in regard to the recurrent trouble spots in Northern Ireland, the answers to these questions are obvious. However, there are area variations in violence in Northern Ireland (Schellenberg, 1977) and the fact is that most of Northern Ireland has been peaceful most of the time since the troubles began, a fact of which people outside the province, in my experience, tend to be unaware or sceptical. Indeed, Cairns, Hunter and Herring (1978) have raised the pointed question as to whether the children in the quiet areas of Northern Ireland are even aware that they are living in what is known to the rest of the world as 'war-torn Ulster'.

Addressing themselves to this question, Cairns, Hunter and Herring (1978) hypothesised, in view of the large amount of time which children are estimated to spend watching television in Britain (Howe, 1977) and the violence-laden content of Northern Irish local news coverage (Blumler, 1971), that television was partially responsible for Northern Irish children's preoccupation with violent events. This hypothesis was tested by comparing two groups of children exposed to Northern Irish television, one group living in an area of Scotland's west coast which can only receive Northern Irish television, the other from a virtually trouble-free area of Northern Ireland, with a control group from a Glasgow suburb where Northern Irish television cannot be received.

Younger children in the study (five to six year olds), were asked to respond as they saw fit to ambiguous picture stimuli, for example, a row of derelict houses. Older children (seven to eight year olds) were asked to write an essay entitled 'Here is the news'. There were almost two hundred children involved in the study and the results showed clearly the influence of Northern Irish television.

Younger Scottish children within Northern Ireland's television range made much more mention of bombs and explosions than their Glasgow counterparts. In the small Scottish island town where some subjects were seen, and where television may have been a particularly important source of entertainment, the younger children were every bit as aware as their Northern Irish counterparts of bombs and explosions, despite their literal insulation. The pattern was similar with older Scottish children's essays, the quintessential response being given by one young essayist with typical Caledonian brevity—'a bomb has just gone of [sic] in Belfast and that is the end of the news'. Furthermore, there was evidence that the actual levels of violence in Northern Ireland, reflected inevitably in television news coverage, quantitively altered the conflict-related content of children's responses accordingly. This was true whether the children lived in Northern Ireland or not.

An important question, which these findings raise, as far as children are concerned, is whether this exposure to and assimilation of television news coverage in Ulster leads to a greater acceptance of violence as usual and acceptable. Russell's (1973) findings would suggest that this may be the case to some extent with Northern Irish children in regard to political violence, notwithstanding the signs of equivocation noted in his data.

A group of studies has been concerned with the attitudes of Northern Irish young people to society, to social issues and to each other. Ed Cairns of the New University of Ulster, has been directing his attention to the development of ethnic consciousness in relation to outgroups in Northern Irish children and has uncovered a number of interesting phenomena.

Cairns and Duriez (1976) showed that ten and eleven year old Protestant and Catholic primary schoolchildren, in a small town relatively unaffected by the troubles, were differentially retentive of information tape-recorded to them by speakers with different accents. Catholic children had a tendency to 'switch off' at a standard English RP accent (roughly, a 'posh' BBC accent) and Protestant children were similarly affected by a middle class Dublin accent. This study gives a fascinating insight into the processes by which divergent cognitions can result despite identical cognitive inputs. More particularly, as the authors respectfully noted '. . . the results may have important implications . . . for teachers and politicians with RP accents when attempting to communicate to certain sections of the Northern Irish community.' (p. 442)

In Northern Ireland, many adults would claim to be able to identify the religion of strangers with a reasonable degree of success simply from a knowledge of their names (Lloyd, 1976). Indeed this ability is celebrated in song, a couplet of a Protestant version of a popular song running —'If your name is Timothy or Pat, you'll never get into Ulster with a Fenian name like that'. Pursuing this idea with first names, Lloyd (1976) found with a group of eighty-eight Irish subjects that Catholic names, as the song would suggest, are particularly 'visible' in this respect. Six first names were listed by over 50 per cent of the subjects as being 'most typical of' Catholics (Patrick, Sean, Seamus, Mary, Bridget and Bernadette) while only one 'Protestant' name emerged in this criterion (William).

Reviewing a number of studies carried out at the New University of Ulster, Cairns (in press) found that the development of this discriminatory capacity is a relatively slow process, with the majority of children not showing evidence of categorizing names in this way until they are approximately eleven years old. This contrasts with the development of racial discriminatory capacities in American studies which seem to appear much earlier.

These studies indicate that Northern Irish children become sensitive to quite subtle discriminatory cues related to their religion and national identity. Taking this fact, and the time-scale of the development of ethnic discrimination in Northern Ireland, Cairns has argued that ethnic discrimination in Northern Ireland is a much more complex process than racial discrimination as perceived in research conducted in the United States. For example, Northern Irish children do not seem to be generally prejudiced against other social groups (such as negroes) even though they are prejudiced against their local outgroups (Protestants or Catholics). As Jahoda and Harrison (1975) note : 'The outgroup antagonism characteristic of Belfast children is thus seen to be highly specialised and compatible with tolerance in other directions.' (p. 8)

Jahoda and Harrison's (1975) study in which children from the Shankill-Falls area of Belfast were compared with a control group of Edinburgh children from a poor working class area also used an indirect means of assessing attitudes. In this case, preference patterns to linear drawings dressed to represent various roles of interest to the researchers (e.g. soldier, priest) were elicited. The results showed a general Belfast antipathy towards the police, more marked among Catholic children, a distinctly unfavourable attitude towards soldiers among Belfast Catholic children and, in regard to the roles of Roman Catholic priest and Protestant minister, a strong antagonism towards the outgroup figure on the part of the Belfast children.

But within the context of Northern Irish affairs, there is really nothing surprising in these attitudes towards violence and outgroups. A detailed interview study by Adelson (1971) of 450 adolescents from the United States, Germany and Britain, aged eleven to eighteen of both sexes, showed that young adolescents generally have little sense of society, little ability to decentre and put themselves in the other man's shoes, even when the other man is a hypothetical person on a hypothetical island. Young adolescents in Adelson's study emerged as frequently authoritarian, even bloodthirsty, for example positing harsher and harsher punishments as solutions to law-breaking. Moral absolutism is the order of the day at this age. In some respects, the problem of Northern Irish society is not that there is anything peculiar about the attitudes of Northern Irish youngsters under the circumstances, but that such attitudes so frequently appear to persist into adulthood.

However, even this judgment may be harsh. A study by Schmidt (1960) of schoolchildren in Britain, Israel, Germany and Switzerland provided evidence that historical hatreds, even in the absence of current animosities, are the norm. Schmidt concluded that group loyalty itself 'is often responsible for irrational, unhealthy social animosity' (p. 257) and pinpointed the directing influence of the animosity as the home primarily, but also the media and the populist ploys of political leaders. These ideas have a familiar ring in the Ulster context, but it should be emphasised that Schmidt's studies were carried out in the 1950s totally without reference to the Irish situation.

Although Protestants and Catholics in Ulster do not constitute separate nations in any strict political sense, their separate education, versions of history, cultural activities, religious habits, residential patterns and political viewpoints provide sufficient basis to justify a comparison with cross-national studies, without implying any evaluation of two-nations theories (e.g. British and Irish Communist Organisation, 1971). And the fact is that other cross-cultural work has confirmed the general drift of Schmidt's argument that the development of such animosities and preferences is quite normal in children (Tajfel and Jahoda, 1966; Tajfel et al, 1970; Middleton, Tajfel and Johnson, 1970).

In some ways, the single most important question which has been raised about Northern Ireland is that of the effect of the troubles on Northern Irish youth, and in particular on those most closely involved in or exposed to communal forms of anti-social behaviour. At its most basic, the question is whether the experiences of the children and adolescents of Northern Ireland have left them resistant to the control of law or indeed any control, and whether they will create havoc in Ulster, even in the event of a political solution being found. Lyons (1973b) and Fraser (1973) have indicated on the basis of their early clinical contacts with children from strife-torn areas that indeed this gloomy scenario is likely to be enacted. From the quite different perspective of experience and research in Northern Irish training schools, Curran, Jardine and Harbison (in press) have come to much the same conclusion, expressing the fear that 'when peace and stability return, problems of anti-social behaviour among the young may emerge as a major feature of life.'

On the face of it, the evidence is that there are substantial grounds for such fears. The previously noted social conditions in Northern Ireland are almost all prominent among correlates of delinquency (West and Farrington 1973). Jardine, Curran and Harbison (1978) note that official statistics show that the number of indictable offences known to the police rose from 15,000 in 1967 to almost 40,000 in 1976. There are, however, as these authors note, problems with the validity of official statistics on crime and delinquency as indicators of the actual levels of crime and delinquency in a given society. But several investigations have yielded data on variables typically associated with delinquency and which may therefore provide alternative sources of information on likely current or potential levels of delinquency in Ulster.

All groups of delinquents have a poor record of school attendance (Wadesworth, 1975). A survey of truancy in the Belfast and North East Education and Library Board areas (*Report of the Interdepartmental Committee on Matters Relating to the Alienation of Young People*, 1974) found that rates of absence increased by between 40 per cent and 109 per cent during the years 1966 to 1974. This survey also found that unusually high rates of absenteeism were an urban phenomenon associated with inner-city areas and working class housing estates in Belfast. Caven and Harbison's (in press) recent survey confirms this, finding Belfast and Londonderry particularly high on absenteeism.

It would seem, therefore, that some areas of Northern Ireland, at least, have a truancy problem of serious proportions and, by implication, a delinquency problem. Boal (1974), in his study of the Belfast urban area, found that almost 18 per cent of children and young people brought before the court were under control orders in which educational problems were cited. A recent study of one of the two male training schools in Northern Ireland by the Statistics and Economics Unit of the Department of Finance, Northern Ireland (*Research Report*, 1976) suggested that over 20 per cent of boys were committed for mainly educational offences.

Reading retardation and anti-social behaviour are also strongly correlated (Rutter, Tizard and Whitmore, 1970; Sturge, 1972). The Areas of Special Need Study (1977) found on testing all P7 (eleven-year-old) children in the Belfast urban area for reading retardation that 26 per cent were classified as retarded. This study also found that reading retardation was the highest correlate of the spatial distribution of juvenile delinquency, correlating at $+0.64$.

Some studies have used psychometric techniques to assess the extent of anti-social attitudes or characteristics in Northern Irish children. Russell (1973), as we have noted, found that 50 to 60 per cent of primary schoolboys and 60 to 70 per cent of secondary schoolboys thought it acceptable to use violence for political ends. Fee (1976) examined teacher's ratings of over 5,000 Belfast children's behaviour using a questionnaire devised by Rutter (Rutter, Tizard and Whitmore, 1970) and found Belfast children to be high on anti-social behaviour. Comparing these findings with those of similar studies in London and the Isle of Wight (Rutter, Tizard and Whitmore, 1970; Sturge, 1972) he found that, while London children appear to experience twice the rate of neurotic disturbance as do either Belfast or Isle of Wight children, on the measure of anti-social behaviour, the Belfast children were higher than the London children and considerably higher than the Isle of Wight sample.

Recent studies by the Northern Ireland Training Schools Research Group (Curran, Jardine and Harbison, in press; Jardine, Curran and Harbison, 1978) have compared Northern Irish and other British normal schoolboys and delinquent boys on various scales of the Jessness Inventory, an American instrument designed to classify delinquents and disturbed adolescents. The most valid comparison in these studies is with recently tested Scottish boys and the results showed that Northern Irish Training School boys and normal schoolboys tend to have more deviant characteristics than their Scottish counterparts.

All of this evidence taken together appears to make a prima facie case for the assumption of future problems of anti-social behaviour among the youth of Northern Ireland. And yet, there are problems in taking it at face value, both in the specific terms of the studies cited and in relation to larger, more general issues within the situation in Northern Ireland.

First, as Jardine, Curran and Harbison (1978) note, the number of indictable offences known to the police in Northern Ireland is still only two-thirds of the rate in England and Wales despite ten years of social turmoil. If one looks at the figures presented by these authors for juveniles found guilty per thousand of the juvenile population, then Northern Ireland's rate is similarly two-thirds the rate in England and Wales for all offences and only one-third for indictable offences. However, there are differences in legislation which render indictable/non-indictable distinctions problematical for comparative purposes.

It is true that such statistics are unreliable generally and it is frequently assumed that Northern Irish statistics are somewhat more problematical than most as valid indicators of real levels of crime and delinquency. In regard to conviction statistics, this argument may have some force. However it is not unreasonable to argue that in regard to the official statistics on the total number of offences known to the police, the Northern Irish statistics are likely to be reasonably accurate. One might reasonably assume that with the strenuous RUC and British Army intelligence efforts in the province, relatively little is missed in comparison to other areas of the United Kingdom, although for the purposes of this discussion 'known' offences do not relate specifically or exclusively to juvenile offences. More generally it does not seem reasonable to ignore hard evidence on the unverified assumption that one set of unspecifiable distorting factors is possibly more important than another set of unspecifiable distorting factors.

The link between reading retardation and juvenile delinquency in Northern Ireland found by the Areas of Special Need Study (1977) also needs careful interpretation. The correlation of +0·64 found here was between levels of reading retardation and levels of delinquency in a given area, not between levels of reading retardation and prevalence of delinquency in a given group of subjects. The correlation between the two variables in this study is therefore even more tenuous and incapable of causative or even predictive analysis than such levels of correlation usually are.

Similarly if we examine the comparisons between Scottish and Northern Irish groups of delinquent and normal boys made by the Northern Ireland Training Schools Research Group, we find that of fifteen possible comparisons, eight show no significant differences, in one comparison Scottish boys appear to be more deviant than Northern Irish boys and of the remaining six differences in which Northern Irish boys appear more deviant, only three of these show a mean difference of more than one scale point. Given the acknowledged problems of comparability of samples from different studies and that no details have yet been published of the Scottish sample, it would be unwise to jump to conclusions on the basis of this evidence alone.

More generally, however, there are problems with studies which look at cold statistics without a constant awareness of the political situation from which these statistics emerge. It is rather like putting the cart before the horse to look at aspects of deviance among the province's youth and to extrapolate from these predictions about the future shape of society in Northern Ireland. A more coherent and ecologically valid picture may emerge by setting such statistics firmly in the context of the circumstances from which they derive.

For example, the statistics on school absenteeism (Caven and

Harbison, in press) are most parsimoniously explained by reference to such variables as children's and parents' fears about the
journey to school, children's fears about the safety of their
parents in their absence, the involvement of children in conflict-
related problems and so forth. Indeed the statistics show that :
(a) it is in the areas of greatest conflict, particularly Belfast and
Londonderry, that absenteeism is at its worst; (b) children in the
fifteen- to sixteen-year-old group, in other words those most
likely to be conscious of the dangers of their parents, their community and themselves in their absence at school, are most prone
to absenteeism; (c) in the majority of unjustified absences (57
per cent), there was evidence of parental implication in encouraging the child to be absent and (d) almost half of unjustified
absenteeism (45 per cent) is accounted for by girls who are much
less likely than boys to become involved in delinquent acts. This
would not appear to be typical, potentially delinquent, truancy.

Again those studies which have measured various characteristics of Northern Irish youth in the post-1969 period have made
two implicit assumptions. First, that high levels of indices which
are known to be correlated with anti-social behaviour in other
societies have arisen as a result of experience during the troubles.
Second, that these indices are predictive in the Northern Irish
context of future anti-social behaviour.

The problem with the former of these assumptions is that we
have no base-line data, no pre-1969 data against which to test
this assumption. In other words, it may well be that had Northern
Irish children been tested prior to the present troubles, they
would also have appeared high on correlates of anti-social behaviour, such as Jessness Inventory scales. Certainly, one would
be surprised, if for example, Belfast children had appeared any
more 'soft' or less tough than their counterparts in Glasgow or
London, troubles or no troubles. And the Jessness Inventory
Scales used in the Training Schools Research Group studies are
in some sense at least, measures of toughness in the colloquial
sense.

This leads rather naturally to the latter assumption of these
studies that these indices will predict future anti-social behaviour
in Northern Ireland. It seems entirely reasonable to suppose that,
given their known validity in other societies, they will also be
predictive of anti-social behaviour in Northern Ireland. The

more important question which appears to have been overlooked is *how* predictive they are in the Northern Irish context. The hard evidence shows that despite, for example, high levels of teacher-rated anti-social behaviour in Belfast school children and despite high scores on Jessness Inventory Scales predictive of anti-social tendencies, the actual rates of delinquency in Northern Ireland are considerably below those in England and Wales.

Indeed, accepted correlates of crime and delinquency have never been very good predictors in Northern Ireland. For example, despite some of the worst social conditions in the United Kingdom, or indeed, Europe, Northern Ireland has been an area of relatively low levels of crime and delinquency generally; this is particularly evident when one looks at serious crime. One of the most startling statistics about Northern Ireland, particularly in retrospect, is that in 1965 there was one murder in the entire year in the province. At no time during the 1960s prior to 1969 did the total number of murders reach double figures.

The most likely syndrome which accounts for this peculiarly Northern Irish phenomenon is the strength of the churches' influence and the fundamentalist religious values espoused by both Roman Catholics and Protestants in Ulster (Rose, 1971). This syndrome entails a degree of respect for, or at least compliance with the authority of elders uncommon in the British Isles. Some authors, for example, Lyons (1973b), have simply asserted that respect for authority has broken down completely although this assertion remains unsubstantiated. Other observers with noses rather closer to the ground, have taken the opposing view that, in fact, mutual respect has increased as young and old have become involved in the problems of their community (Jenvey, 1972; Overy, 1972; Foley, 1973).

Jardine, Curran and Harbison (1978) have made the point that as in England and Wales, the vast majority of juvenile indictable offences are 'crimes of dishonesty' and that political crimes constitute a relatively small proportion of all offences. Indeed, taking this comparison a little further, the correlation co-efficient between the total number of indictable offences known to the police in Northern Ireland and in England and Wales between 1967 and 1976 turns out to be +0.93, indicating a surprisingly close relationship between trends in crime and delinquency on both sides of the water during recent years. Furthermore, a similar calculation between the official statistics of Northern Ireland and the Republic of Ireland during the years 1968 to 1977 reveals a correlation of +0·96. Again, this is an astonishingly high correlation and indicates that (*a*) criminal trends throughout the British Isles in recent years appear to have fluctuated for much the same reasons, whatever they are and (*b*) the troubles in Northern Ireland have had very little overall effect on criminality in the province (unless we entertain the unlikely possibility that the troubles in Northern Ireland closely influence criminal trends throughout the British Isles).

Having said that, however, there is evidence of a need to distinguish between politically motivated and other juvenile offenders. Elliott and Lockhart (in press) show that despite the remarkably similar socio-economic backgrounds of juvenile scheduled offenders and 'ordinary' juvenile delinquents, scheduled offenders are more intelligent, have higher educational attainments, show less evidence of early developmental problems and have fewer previous court appearances than juvenile delinquents.

It would, therefore, seem that fears of a consequent boom in anti-social behaviour among Northern Irish youth, even in the event of a political settlement, are largely unjustified. The sum total of the problem will be represented by the degree to which rates of crime and delinquency in Northern Ireland exceed corresponding rates elsewhere in the British Isles. The current evidence, when set in the context of traditional Ulster social patterns and the political situation in the province, would suggest that that excess may be considerably less than has been imagined. It may even be non-existent.

The whole question of attitudes to violence, attitudes to social groups and issues and respect for authority raises, rather naturally, the issue of the underlying values from which the attitudes emanate. A recent study by McKernan (in press) has looked at the relative importance of a variety of values for a large group (751) of fourth year secondary school pupils in the counties of Londonderry and Antrim. The sample was quite well balanced in terms of religion, sex, rural/urban environment, social class and school type.

McKernan looked at instrumental values (means) and terminal values (ends) using the method put forward by Rokeach (1973).

Subjects are asked to rank in order of subjective importance eighteen terminal values (e.g. happiness, self-respect, a world of beauty) and eighteen instrumental values (e.g. ambitious, courageous, loving).

The most important terminal values for both Protestant and Catholic children were a world at peace, freedom and happiness. The most important instrumental values for both groups were honest, clean and loving. The overall picture is of a relatively idealised set of values with, appropriately and encouragingly, a desire for peace prominent among them. Interestingly, the terminal value salvation, the most explicitly religious value, is ranked very low by both groups of children. Although this might appear odd, given the high religiosity in Northern Ireland (Rose, 1971), the religious concept of 'being saved' at a specific watershed in one's life, is associated in Ulster with some minority Protestant sects and is probably, therefore, denominationally foreign to both the majority of Protestants and Catholics.

In terms of instrumental values, the Christian values honest and loving obtain prominence and underline the influence of the churches and parents in Ulster in promoting values consonant with the Christian ethic. Also among the first half of the instrumental values ranked by both Protestant and Catholic children are the Christian values forgiving, helpful and responsible.

There are some interesting and significant differences between Protestant and Catholic children in the order of importance which they attach to terminal values. Although both groups value freedom highly, Catholic children place this value first in their hierarchy of values while Protestant children place it third (they place a world at peace first). This difference is statistically significant ($p < 0.001$). Catholic children also value equality higher (sixth in rank) than Protestant children (eleventh in rank). Again the difference is statistically significant ($p < 0.001$).

This result supports the view put forward in Chapter Two that the real problem Catholics have with their position in Ulster is political. The pre-eminence of the value freedom shown in McKernan's study contrasts starkly with the fact that no Catholic in Rose's (1971) study mentioned freedom as a characteristic liked about his church, whereas 29 per cent of Protestants mentioned it specifically, the largest category endorsement. Rokeach

(1973) has reported that equality is a value that has repeatedly been found to differentiate ideological positions; American blacks, for example, rate equality higher than American whites.

Can anything be done to change attitudes among children or to prevent the development of attitudes which have led to the characteristically intransigent positions of group leaders in Northern Ireland? This question is central to the debate on integrated education in Ulster. Much has been written and said in this debate and I do not intend to go over old ground in this discussion. Akenson (1973) has given a thorough account of the history of the problem in the province.

The bare facts are that Catholics are educated in 'voluntary' schools, largely government financed but essentially controlled by the Catholic Church which ensures that its children receive an appropriate slice of religious education and learn about their Irish heritage and culture. Barritt and Carter (1961) estimate that 98 per cent of Catholic children are educated separately.

Protestants are educated in wholly state-financed schools in which religious education is considerably less in quantity and is based on notionally non-denominational Bible study which, in fact, reflects a pan-Protestant approach to religious instruction. Protestant children are taught British history and cultural values, with little emphasis on the historical problems of Ireland and the Irish. Indeed in British historical texts, Ireland and the Irish are frequently presented as merely a fleeting British problem.

The Catholic Church is more open in its defence of separate education (Conway, 1970) and in its efforts to ensure that the system of non-sectarian, non-religious education, envisioned by Lord Londonderry at the inception of the state of Northern Ireland in 1921, did not come into being. However, the Protestant ecclesiastical community and political leadership, while making political capital out of the Catholic attitude, were very happy to accommodate it and ensure that state schools were, in fact, Protestant schools in which Protestant children were taught by Protestant teachers.

Not only are the children segregated in this way, but most teachers, unless they attend university or polytechnic (which are not segregated) never formally mix with teachers of other religion, since the teacher training colleges are essentially either Catholic or Protestant. At least half of the teachers even belong to what are, in fact, segregated unions (Robinson, 1971; Arnold and Clarke, 1971).

One of the most peculiar aspects of this peculiar state of affairs is that it does not represent the wishes of the public, or at least it did not represent public opinion just before the present troubles. A survey by the *Belfast Telegraph* in 1968, confirmed by Rose (1971), showed that between 60 and 70 per cent of both Catholics and Protestants favoured integrated education.

The most vehement defence of segregated education is put forward by the hierarchy of the Catholic Church, who regard the religious aspect of education as absolutely essential in protecting the faith of future generations (Conway, 1970). The desire for integrated education is seen not as a positive desire for harmony among the people of Ulster, but dismissed as an example of 'the current wave of secularism' (Bishop Philbin in 1967).

Two implicit arguments in the integrated education debate are that (*a*) since political discord predates segregated education, then it cannot be regarded as a contributory cause of discord in Ulster and (*b*) since the absence of integrated education did not cause the problem, then the introduction of integrated education will not solve it.

In regard to the former of these arguments, in fact, there are very sound psychological reasons for supposing that the institution of segregated education is a contributory factor to intergroup hostility and disaffection in Ulster. I will elaborate these reasons below. The latter argument can be dismissed with somewhat less ceremony for, although at first glance it appears tautologous, it is, in fact, a non-sequitur. Applied, for example, to the field of medicine, the argument would lead one to conclude that since the lack of penicillin does not cause disease, then its administration to patients cannot cure disease.

The first point that must be made in regard to integrated education is that it is naïve to assume that simply integrating schools will solve the problems of Northern Ireland overnight. The questions we must ask are (*a*) what are the likely effects of such a move in the relatively short-term say, when the system has been in operation for five years, and (*b*) what effect would this move have on the long-term total picture of inter-group feeling in Northern Ireland?

There is considerable evidence that inter-group contact often reduces inter-group hostility and promotes inter-group liking (Stouffer et al., 1949; Amir, 1969; Harding et al., 1969; Pettigrew, 1971). A number of studies have shown low levels of prejudice in contact situations in schools, on the job and in the community (Horowitz, 1936; Brophy, 1945; Deutsch and Collins, 1951; Wilner et al., 1955; Williams, 1964; Hyman and Sheatsley, 1964). However, for some of these studies at least, there existed the possibility that low initial prejudice may have been a factor in the racial contact. There is however, experimental evidence which shows that contact can cause favourable attitudes. Mann (1959), for example, assigned blacks and whites to six-person discussion groups and found that over successive meetings, members of the groups became less sensitive to racial barriers.

However, contact alone will not reduce prejudice. To take but one example, slave owners in the Southern States of the United States of America had considerable contact with black people, but were much more prejudiced than people in the Northern States, many of whom had never seen a black person. Studies of school segregation and racial attitudes in the United States generally yield inconsistent results. Some have found increased prejudice, some have found reduced prejudice and some have found no change (Clark, 1953; Pettigrew, 1961). In addition, it seems that contact can reduce prejudice in a specific setting without producing a more generalised reduction of prejudice in other settings. Minard (1952), for example, found that even though blacks and whites in a Southern United States coal mine worked amicably side by side underground, they maintained separate lives during off-duty hours.

However, one can press the analogy between American racial and Ulster religious prejudice and discrimination only so far. There are very sound reasons for believing that there are substantially more differences than similarities in the comparisons and that black-white discrimination more readily arises and is more difficult to combat.

Most importantly, as Cairns (in press) has pointed out, the development of ethnic discrimination in Northern Ireland is based on the gradual development of stereotyped cues unlike the development of racial discrimination which involves the use of more simple, purely perceptual cues. In other words, as Katz

(1973) has commented, one would have to be colour blind not to notice the difference between blacks and whites. However, in the absence of such obvious discriminatory cues, more subtle cues have to be learned, and discriminations reinforced to produce the sorts of stereotypes which Catholics and Protestants eventually use to discriminate each other. (I am here using the term 'discriminate' in its purely cognitive sense of 'distinguish between'.)

Overlapping this ability to discriminate, is the whole process of developing attitudes towards outgroup members, which has raised the issue of whether these processes proceed in tandem (Katz, 1976) or whether the ability to discriminate precedes the development of prejudiced attitudes (Katz and Seavey, 1973). Cairns (in press) has made the interesting observation that since the whole chain of events is telescoped in the United States, for example, by the relatively simple process of racial discrimination, there may be much more value in studying the more slowly unfolding non-racial prejudice of Northern Ireland. Nonetheless, the central importance of the role of discriminatory abilities in ethnic attitude development is beyond question (Katz and Zalk, 1974; Tajfel, 1969).

However, these differences between the phenomena of racial prejudice development in the United States and ethnic prejudice in Northern Ireland are not merely of academic interest. They call into question the whole validity of comparing educational integration in the United States with any future integrated system of education in Northern Ireland. American integration, quite apart from the racial aspect discussed above, has had problems which do not or need not arise in Northern Ireland.

Both Clark (1953) and Pettigrew (1961) have argued that problems of group interaction have arisen in desegregation where ambiguous or inconsistent policies are apparent. Clearly, therefore, in the light of this knowledge, it should not be impossible, given the right professional advice, for ambiguities and inconsistencies in any proposed system of integration to be anticipated and avoided in Northern Ireland.

One important difference with fundamental ramifications is that in the United States, non-white children are very much in the minority. According to the 1970 United States census, the non-white population was only 25,463,000 compared to a white population of 177,749,000. This poses two distinct problems for non-white children: they are undeniably different and in a clear minority. In other words it is they who have to be integrated into society as a whole. Black separatists would argue the morally tenable but practically unhelpful case that racism is a white problem and that whites should solve it among themselves (Pettigrew, 1971). In Northern Ireland, however, such difficulties do not arise. Although the Catholic/Protestant population ratio is still roughly 35/65, the school population ratio has been approaching 50/50 in recent years.

The net effect of all these differences is that there are grounds for optimism about the effect of school integration in Northern Ireland despite equivocal indications from studies on integration in the United States.

One of the effects of an integrated school system would be to retard the development of the process of ethnic discrimination which Cairns (in press) has described. Ulster children, by age eleven, seem, for example, to have developed a familiarity with their own religious group's names to the extent that they are as unfamiliar with typical names among the other religious group as they are with 'foreign' names. Integration would make serious inroads into such key contributory mechanisms in the development of outgroup hostility and prejudice.

However, we have noted that contact per se, integrated education per se, is not sufficient to bring about a radical and pervasive reduction in inter-group hostility. What circumstances, therefore, must attend integrated education in order that the interaction which it entails may lead to a more general reduction in inter-group prejudice in Ulster? Allport (1954), in a classic contribution to the understanding of prejudice, has outlined four such conditions.

First, equality of status is important. MacKenzie (1948) found that among white American war veterans, only 5 per cent of those who had contact with unskilled, low-status blacks had favourable interracial attitudes, whereas 64 per cent of the veterans who had contact with skilled, professional, high-status blacks expressed favourable interracial attitudes. We have already noted that reasonable parity of numbers within the system is now the case. Status, in any case, would be less of a problem among children unless the system created its own problems of this kind. For example, it would be unwise to ignore the balance of numbers and status between Protestants and Catholics in a given school. Ideally, every school, irrespective of the Protestant/Catholic ratio of its intake, should have teachers of both religions with an appropriate apportionment of grades, reflecting no religious bias in status among staff.

The second and third conditions, which Allport posited as necessary to reduce prejudice through contact, were that the two groups should be seeking common goals and co-operating to reach these goals. In the Ulster situation, there are a variety of levels at which this can be interpreted. At the quite literal level, common goals could be sought through common sports. At present, Protestant children tend to play 'English' games—rugby, soccer, cricket and so forth. Catholic children tend to play 'Irish' games such as gaelic football, hurling and camogie. In an integrated system, inter-school competitive prowess in any of these sports would tend to generate pride, common interest and support among pupils within the school generally, even though, initially at least, Protestant and Catholic children might tend to participate in their 'own' sports. In much the same way on a national level, Olympic success in minority sports such as small-bore rifle shooting, decathlon or shot-putting can generate national pride and interest.

At another level, the study of common subjects, particularly history, would contribute towards the same objective. Catholic education in history is heavily oriented towards Irish history with an inevitable Republican bias, while Protestants study British history and, if at all, Irish history as seen by British historians. This is an area where a common, balanced approach might well exorcise some political banshees, place the burden of fact on ethnic myth and generally tint the chasm between the respective blacks and whites with the appropriate shades of grey. The result might well provide a more solid basis for mutual understanding and shared pride.

Finally, contact is likely to lead to a reduction in prejudice if that contact is consistent with prevailing laws, customs and traditions. In regard to the former, post-1969 legislation aimed at removing Catholic grievances has now been enacted although emergency legislation aimed at controlling the security situation remains a Catholic grievance. The question of customs and traditions is more vexed however. Clearly, in one sense integrated education is directly contrary to customs and traditions. Yet new customs and traditions have to start somewhere and the evidence of the 1968–69 polls mentioned previously, was that the people of Ulster, Catholic and Protestant, wished to change their customs and traditions at least as far as denominational education was concerned.

In a sense, this final condition set forth by Allport is the 'crunch' issue, for a school experience, which is at odds with experience elsewhere, will be consequently that much less effective than it would otherwise be. Some commentators have made the mistaken inference that in such circumstances, integrated education would make no difference whatsoever. Maurice Hayes, ex-Chairman of the now-defunct Community Relations Commission is quoted as saying that 'an edict in the morning integrating schools would not make a button of difference' (*Fortnight*, 1973b, p. 8). In the short-term, this view might prove correct; in the long-term, however, there are sound reasons for doubting it.

A fundamental premise in social psychology is that people prefer, if possible, to behave in ways consistent with their stated or felt positions in regard to social issues and objects (their attitudes and values) and alternatively, that people prefer to feel that their attitudes and values are consistent with their behaviour. A huge volume of research has been concerned with this drive towards consistency and various mechanisms have been proposed by which individuals theoretically adjust cognitions (including cognitions of their own behaviour) to yield a comfortable state of cognitive consistency (Heider, 1946; Newcomb, 1953; Osgood and Tannenbaum, 1955; Festinger, 1957; Abelson and Rosenberg, 1958). The behavioural phenomena which give rise to these theories have also been interpreted as indicating a drive towards consistency with one's self-image (Bem, 1967).

It is in this context that one can appreciate what the psychological effect of segregated education has been on society at large. It has, in some degree, confirmed those opposed to any institutionalised rapprochement between Catholics and Protestants in their attitudes. Their behaviour (i.e. sending their children to segregated schools) has been perfectly consistent with their attitudes. On the other hand, for those whose attitudes and values would lead them to favour integrated education, the act of sending their children to segregated schools has been inconsistent with

F

their beliefs. On theoretical grounds, one would suspect that those most marginally committed to such attitudes and values would regain consistency by altering their attitudes and values to embrace segregated education.

On the other hand, were integrated education to be introduced, the 'silent majority' would be reinforced in their attitudes and values. Those, whose views are most entrenched, would find themselves in an uncomfortable state of inconsistency, sending their children to schools in which they will mix with the children of the group to which they are opposed.

In order to regain consistency, a number of theoretical options are open to them. They could adjust their attitudes and values to include integrated education, although this would not occur readily in people of such strong views. They could, on the other hand, decide that since they are 'forced' by the State to educate their children in integrated schools, then this is not really inconsistent with their attitudes and values and hence, they could retain these reasonably intact. Much the same mechanism is probably now in operation among those who favour integrated education and yet are 'forced' to send their children to segregated schools. In the latter case, the Catholic Church is more likely to be seen as the culprit. However, in this latter instance, the group favouring integrated education is in the clear majority if polls are any indication. If integrated education were to be introduced as the State system in Northern Ireland, then those opposed to it would have to find a way of rationalising their behaviour. The churches, by reappraising their dogmatic approach to education, could act as a strong force for social change in this instance. If they gave their backing to an integrated system, then this would seriously weaken the foundations of the attitudes held by the most bigoted and hostile sections of Northern Irish society.

So, on these premises, it can be seen that the very fact of segregated education has been a factor in preventing movement in attitudes among adults in Northern Ireland. By the same token, the very fact of integrated education will release forces for change in attitudes among adults, particularly parents, even if only, in some cases to drive hardened attitudes onto more perilous foundations in the short-term.

Cardinal Conway (1970) put forward a reasoned defence of Catholic education in Northern Ireland, in particular drawing attention to the experience of countries such as Great Britain, Holland and the United States where a similar Catholic approach to education has caused no particular problems of the kind experienced in Northern Ireland. But while Cardinal Conway's pamphlet would, I imagine, make unobjectionable reading in those places, or even in the Republic of Ireland, it is precisely because Northern Ireland is different, with its own peculiar problems, that the usual approach of the Catholic Church to education is inappropriate there. Cardinal Conway was right to argue that segregated education did not cause the problem of inter-group tension in Northern Ireland but, as I have argued, it is quite illogical to argue from that premise that integrated education could not contribute to a solution of the problem.

It is unfortunate that the powers that be in Northern Ireland appear to view comprehensive education (in which pupils of all abilities are taught under one roof in the American High School manner) to be a more important priority than integrated education. The report of the Advisory Council for Education, published in 1973 and entitled *Reorganisation of Secondary Education in Northern Ireland*, specifically recommended the move towards comprehensive education. Its chairman, as *Fortnight* (1973c) notes, when presenting the report to the press 'implied that integration was the myopic panacea of an idealistic liberal fringe' (p. 8).

In England the comprehensive education debate has been presented to some considerable extent as a clash of social classes. By and large it has been the wealthier end of society which has had access to the 'best' educational establishments, despite the intentions of successive governments. However, Northern Irish people, as we have seen in Chapter Two, are curiously lacking in class consciousness. It is in this context that one finds it difficult to avoid the suspicion, notwithstanding the strength of the educational arguments for comprehensive education, that the rush towards a comprehensive system represents an earnest but nonetheless misguided and inappropriate desire for change in the Northern Irish educational system. In a nutshell, comprehensive education per se represents the importation of an English cure for which there is no known Northern Irish disease.

Given the importance of a milieu in the extra-school environment in which children encounter the minimum possible number of conflicts with their experiences in school, perhaps it would be appropriate to conclude this examination of the issues in integrated education by noting that a move to integrated education could begin now. The recent review of political opinion surveys in Northern Ireland by Rose and his colleagues (1978) revealed that direct rule is the most generally acceptable political solution (within Northern Ireland) of all the solutions presently available. This would suggest that present political circumstances, vacuous as they are, offer a context with the minimum number of ideological conflicts in which an integrated system of education could begin to contribute to improved inter-group relations in Northern Ireland.

Finally, it would serve us well to remember two points in regard to Northern Irish children. First, as Taylor and Nelson (1977) have pointed out, there is a need at this point to consider changes over time since 1969. When considering young people, it is not only circumstances which change with the years, but the entire subject population.

Second, we must consider changes over location. It is a matter of record that there are area variations in unemployment rates, emigration rates, levels of ill-health and housing standards. Equally, there are marked differences by area of the level and frequency of violence to which young people have been exposed (Schellenberg, 1977). Furthermore, many commentators have pointed out from experience that there are area variations in the strength and type of local outgroup prejudice or feeling. O'Donnell's (1977) study of stereotypes provides evidence, for example, that Londonderry stereotypes are milder than Belfast stereotypes. We must, therefore, avoid reifying the problems of young people in Northern Ireland and move on from a 1969 Belfast conception of Northern Irish society.

Concluding Comments

I have attempted to illustrate in this analysis some of the important psychological dimensions of the Northern Irish problem and to show how historical, cultural, economic and political influences have created the characteristic psychological ambiance of the province. It follows from the premises on which this analysis rests that future initiatives, either within or beyond Northern Ireland, intended to alleviate the problem or move towards a solution to it must take into account the various psychological effects which would follow in the train of such developments.

A political settlement in Northern Ireland, in this sense, is, therefore, a beginning to a solution of the problem, not an end to it. We have seen in Chapter Two that a political solution could well assuage the fears and grievances of the Catholic community, but could not per se alleviate the deep-seated fear and suspicion which Protestants in Ulster have of the Catholic Church.

Cruise O'Brien (1972) put his finger on a crucial issue when he stated that because of the nature of the constitution of the Irish Republic, Protestants living there became Catholic by nationality. It is, to a lesser extent, true that those who decided to give allegiance to the government of Northern Ireland became Protestant by nationality, the difference being that a significant proportion of Northern Ireland's inhabitants withheld that allegiance (Rose, 1971). Thus, Ulster's Catholics remained in political purgatory.

The assumption that a military victory over terrorist organisations will provide the basis for solving the problem in Northern Ireland is, in fact, only marginally more naïve than the assumption that a politician can somehow wave a magic wand, dip into a bag of political tricks and, hey presto, produce the cure for Ulster's ills. The problem is more complex than that and will require the involvement of rather more people, at all levels, than mere soldiers and politicians.

In particular, the role of the churches in Ireland over the years has been unhelpful at best, given the high degree of religiosity in the country and hence the scope for widespread beneficial influence. Certainly, the platitudes have wafted forth with monotonous regularity, but the prospect of any change within the churches' own attitudes and practices, which could begin the gradual process of reducing suspicion and tension between the two religious communities, has been conspicuous by its absence. Sectional interest and dogmatic rivalry remain the cornerstones of religious authority in Ireland, North and South.

A few examples will serve to illustrate the point. At the General Synod of the Church of Ireland in May 1979, a resolution urging joint (mixed religion) schools in Ireland was dropped because of the threat which such a system would pose to the small and dwindling numerical strength of the Church of Ireland in the Republic. The premise was that the ensuing increased likelihood of intermarriage would result in a diminution in the numbers of Church of Ireland members. To avoid a divisive vote, the resolution was withdrawn (*Irish Times*, 16 May 1979).

The Catholic Church continues to arrogate the right to demand of its members in a mixed marriage the commitment that the children of the marriage be brought up as Catholics. This quite naturally incenses many Ulster Protestants, who regard it as proof of the insidious and all-consuming influence of the Catholic Church, thereby supporting anti-Catholic attitudes. What, they ask, would be our civil rights in a country dominated by an organisation which denies to a parent the right to bring up his or her own children as he or she sees fit? The fact that such inferences may not be objectively justified is beside the point. They are psychologically consistent, are quite predictable in the circumstances and they do happen. No amount of burying one's head in the sand of denominational self-righteousness will change those facts and their consequences.

More recently, the new Moderator of the Presbyterian Church in Ireland, Rev William Craig, has announced that he will not, on grounds of conscience, even speak to the Prelate of the

Catholic Church in Ireland, Archbishop O'Fiaich on doctrinal matters. One could continue ad nauseam with such examples of social irresponsibility and sectional jealousy from the Irish churches. Their investment in helping to solve the problem of inter-community tension in Northern Ireland is circumscribed by their commitment to the maintenance of numerical strength and dogmatic intransigence.

At a social level, the single potentially most helpful step, namely the introduction of integrated schooling, has been avoided, despite the evidence that there would be considerable public support for such a move. Instead, efforts are geared to introducing comprehensive education in this, the least class-conscious area of the United Kingdom. There is no doubt, however, that integrated education would create a new attitudinal climate in Northern Ireland not only in the long-term but also in the relatively short-term and that any serious attempt to tackle the disease of Northern Ireland as opposed to its symptoms could not find a better place to start.

In political terms, interested parties must develop policies and suggest directions which will take into account the likely psychological effect of their proposals on both sections of the community. For example, the government in the Republic of Ireland must, if it is seriously hoping for a rapprochement with the North, assuage Protestant fears of the power and influence of the Catholic Church. The referendum to abolish a clause in the constitution granting special privileges to the Catholic Church (which was carried by a large majority) went some way to achieving this objective. However, while this is a move in a psychologically sound direction, it is really only a beginning.

The recent decision of the Irish government to break the link between Irish pound and sterling, on the other hand, is an example of a move in a psychologically retrograde direction, at least as far as the Northern Irish question is concerned. The Southern pound became 'funny money' in the North. Anyone using it was obviously different and bothersome and the process of travelling and economic communication between the North and South became troublesome and difficult. It was as if, overnight, someone had erected a six-foot wall along the entire length of the North-South border for all to see.

Within a United Kingdom context, the political fears of the

Catholic community that the government is not simply a vehicle for Catholic repression have to be reduced. The greatest escalation in the violence in Northern Ireland arose as a direct result of the introduction of internment. The methods of combating terrorism have now been dressed up in a thin veil of judicial procedure, but the effects are much the same and the Catholic community still feels, with considerable justification, that unjust laws are being unjustly applied. Above all, perhaps, they are aware of the reality, at ground level, of British security forces' behaviour towards the Catholic community and, therefore, many see some justification for the activities of terrorists.

The superego-trip indulged in by the British government that terrorist activities in Northern Ireland are merely criminal not only flies in the face of the objective facts, but is particularly offensive to large sections of the Catholic community, whose version of reality is quite different from that of British government ministers and officials at Westminster and Stormont.

In an Ulster context, the recent proposals by the UDA for an independent Ulster with short-term financial support from Britain is one which has psychological merit, whatever its political and practical difficulties. Most importantly, these proposals envisage a break in the political link with Great Britain, which represents a major political concession to the Catholic community, and asks for a cessation of pressure to join with the Republic of Ireland, which would enable the Protestant community to relax.

In essence, this is a practical example of Osgood's (1962; 1965) suggested psychological approach to conflict resolution, namely 'GRIT' or 'Graduated Reciprocation in Tension-reduction'. In Osgood's proposals, one side announces its intention of making a co-operative, conciliatory gesture. Theoretically, it should be a rather small gesture, so that if it is exploited by the other side, no great harm can ensue. Then follows a period which allows the other side an opportunity to reciprocate the gesture. (At the time of writing we are in this period). If no reciprocation ensues, no great harm has been done. If a reciprocating gesture does occur, this enables the process to continue, leading to the beginning of a trusting relationship between the two parties to the conflict.

Time will tell on this particular proposal but it is certainly a sign that within Northern Ireland there is an awareness of the psychological problems and of the need to tackle them via the medium of creative political initiative. One cannot say the same for either Great Britain or the Republic of Ireland.

Finally, the last word must go to the people of Northern Ireland as they have emerged in this analysis. I have endeavoured to stress the positive as well as the negative aspects of life in Northern Ireland throughout this book. I have not done so merely to minimise the problem but because it is on the strengths of the community and not its weaknesses that the future can be built.

The people of Northern Ireland have suffered much in the past decade but they have come thus far with characteristic human fortitude and resilience in the face of adversity. Despite the prophets of doom, the evidence is that societal norms in Northern Ireland have not deteriorated and will not deteriorate to a level at which peace might be only marginally better than conflict. There remains in Northern Ireland a community of people whose strengths and similarities far outweigh their weaknesses and differences.

F*

Bibliography

Abbott, D. (1973), 'Ian Paisley: evangelism and confrontation in Northern Ireland', *Today's Speech*, 21, 49–55.

Abelson, R. P. and Rosenberg, M. J. (1958), 'Symbolic psychologic: a model of attitudinal cognition', *Behavioural Science*, 3, 1–13.

Abraham, K. (1911), 'Notes on the psychoanalytical investigation and treatment of manic-depressive insanity and allied conditions', in *Selected Papers on Psychoanalysis*, New York: Basic Books, 1960, 137–56.

Adelson, J. (1971), 'The political imagination of the young adolescent', *Daedalus*, 100, 1013–50.

Adorno, T. W., Frenkel-Brunswik, E., Levinson, D. J. and Sanford, R. N. (1950), *The Authoritarian Personality*, New York: Harper.

Advisory Council for Education (1973), *Reorganisation of Secondary Education in Northern Ireland*, Belfast: Her Majesty's Stationery Office.

Akenson, D. H. (1973), *Education and Enmity—Control of Schooling in Northern Ireland, 1920–1950*, Newton Abbot: David and Charles.

Allport, G. W. (1954), *The Nature of Prejudice*, Cambridge, Mass.: Addison-Wesley.

Amir, Y. (1969), 'Contact hypothesis in ethnic relations', *Psychological Bulletin*, 71, 319–42.

Arendt, H. (1963), *Eichmann in Jerusalem: A Report on the Banality of Evil*, New York: Viking Press.

Arnold, S. and Clarke, M. (1971), 'Integration: what about the teachers?' *Fortnight* (15), April 1971, 9–12.

Atkin, T. (1941), 'Air-raid strain in mental hospital admissions', *Lancet*, 2, 72–74.

Aunger, E. A. (1975), 'Religion and occupational class in Northern Ireland', *Economic and Social Review*, 7, 1–18.

Bales, R. F. and Slater, P. E. (1955), 'Role differentiation in small decision-making groups', in T. Parsons et al. (eds), *Family, Socialisation and Interaction Process*, Glencoe, Ill.: Free Press.

Barritt, D. P. and Booth, A. (1972), *Orange and Green—a Quaker Study of Community Relations in Northern Ireland*, Sedbergh (Yorks.) : Northern Friends' Peace Board.

Barritt, D. P. and Carter, C. F. (1972), *The Northern Ireland Problem: A Study in Group Relations* (2nd ed.), London : Oxford University Press.

Basowitz, H., Persky, H., Korchin, S. J. and Grinker, R. R. (1955), *Anxiety and Stress*, New York : McGraw-Hill.

Belfast : Areas of Special Social Need (1977), Belfast : Her Majesty's Stationery Office.

Bell, J. B. (1976), 'Chroniclers of violence in Northern Ireland : a tragedy in endless acts', *Review of Politics*, 38, 510–33.

Bell, J. B. (1978), 'Terror : An Overview', in M. H. Livingston (ed.), *International Terrorism in the Contemporary World*, London : Greenwood Press.

Bem, D. J. (1967), 'Self-perception : an alternative interpretation of cognitive dissonance phenomena', *Psychological Review*, 74, 183–200.

Birrell, D. (1972), 'Relative deprivation as a factor in conflict in Northern Ireland', *Sociological Review*, 20, 317–43.

Bleakley, D. (1974), *Brian Faulkner*, London and Oxford : Mowbrays.

Blumler, J. C. (1971), 'Ulster on the small screen', *New Society*, 18, 1248–50.

Boal, F. W. (1974), *Social Malaise in the Belfast Urban Area*, Belfast : Northern Ireland Community Relations Commission.

Boal, F. W., Doherty, P. and Pringle, D. G. (1974), *The Spatial Distribution of some Social Problems in the Belfast Urban Area*, Belfast : Northern Ireland Community Relations Committee.

Bodman, F. (1941), 'War conditions and the mental health of the child', *British Medical Journal*, 2, 486–8.

Bogardus, E. S. (1925), 'Measuring social distance', *Journal of Applied Sociology*, 9, 299–308.

Bogardus, E. S. (1933), 'A social distance scale', *Sociology and Social Research*, 17, 265–71.

Boulton, D. (1973), *The UVF 1966–1973*, Dublin : Gill & Macmillan.

Bowlby, J. (1952), *Maternal Care and Mental Health*, Geneva : World Health Organisation.

Boyd, A. (1972), *Brian Faulkner and the Crisis of Ulster Unionism*, Tralee : Anvil Books.

British and Irish Communist Organisation (1971), 'On the Democratic Validity of the Northern Ireland State', Belfast.

Brophy, I. N. (1945), 'The luxury of anti-Negro prejudice', *Public Opinion Quarterly*, 9, 456–66.

Brown, F. (1941), Civilian psychiatric air-raid casualties', *Lancet*, 1, 686–91.

Brown, R. (1965), *Social Psychology*, New York : Free Press.

Burbury, W. M. (1941), 'Effects of evacuation and of air-raid on city children', *British Medical Journal*, 2, 660–2.

Burke, P. J. (1972), 'Leadership role differentiation', in C. McClintock (ed.), *Experimental Social Psychology*, New York : Holt, Rinehart & Winston.

Burton, F. (1978), *The Politics of Legitimacy*, London : Routledge & Kegan Paul.

Buss, A. H. (1966), *Psychopathology*, New York : Wiley.

Cairns, E. (in press), 'The development of ethnic discrimination in children in Northern Ireland', in J. I. Harbison and J. J. M. Harbison (eds), *Children and Young People in Northern Ireland*, London : Open Books.

Cairns, E. and Duriez, B. (1976), 'The influence of speaker's accent on recall by Catholic and Protestant school children in Northern Ireland', *British Journal of Social & Clinical Psychology*, 15, 441–2.

Cairns, E., Hunter, D. and Herring, L. (1978), 'Young children's awareness of violence in Northern Ireland : the influence of Northern Irish television in Scotland and Northern Ireland', paper presented to the annual conference of the Northern Ireland Branch of the British Psychological Society at Virginia, Co. Cavan, May 1978.

Calvert, M. (1973), 'The characteristics of guerilla leaders and their rank and file', *The Practitioner*, London, December 1973, n.p.

The Cameron Report (1969), *Disturbance in Northern Ireland: report of the commission Chairman: Lord Cameron*, Cmnd. 532, Belfast : Her Majesty's Stationery Office.

Carroll, F. M. (1978), *American Opinion and the Irish Question 1910–23*, Dublin : Gill & Macmillan.

Caven, N. and Harbison, J. J. M. (in press), 'Persistent school non-attendance : The Northern Ireland situation and the links between non-attendance and some school and socio-economic factors', in J. I. Harbison and J. J. M. Harbison (eds), *Children and Young People in Northern Ireland*, London : Open Books.

Clark, K. B. (1953), 'Desegregation : an appraisal of the evidence', *Journal of Social Issues*, 9, 1–76.

Cleckley, H. (1964), *The Mask of Sanity*, St Louis, Mo. : Mosby.

Clutterbuck, R. (1975), *Living with Terrorism*, London : Faber and Faber.

Clutterbuck, R. (1978), *Britain in Agony: The Growth of Political Violence*, London : Faber and Faber.

Cole, J. (1969), *Introduction to Terence O'Neill, Ulster at the Crossroads*, London : Faber and Faber.

Concannon O'Brien, M. (1979), 'Foreigners' Attitudes Towards Irish People', unpublished doctoral dissertation, Trinity College, Dublin.

Connery, D. (1968), *The Irish*, London : Eyre & Spottiswoode.

Conway, Cardinal William (1970), *Catholic Schools*, Dublin : The Catholic Communications Institute of Ireland, Veritas.

Craft, M. J. (1965), *Ten Studies into Psychopathic Personality*, Bristol : John Wright.

Cruise, O'Brien, C. (1972), *States of Ireland*, London : Panther Books.

Cruise O'Brien, C. (1978), Third Ewart-Biggs Memorial Lecture, delivered at New York University, 30 November 1978.

Curran, J. D., Jardine, E. F. and Harbison, J. J. M. (in press), 'Factors associated with the development of deviant attitudes in Northern Ireland schoolboys', in J. I. Harbison and J. J. M. Harbison (eds), *Children and Young People in Northern Ireland*, London : Open Books.

Darley, J. M. and Latané, B. (1968), 'Bystander intervention in emergencies : diffusion of responsibility', *Journal of Personality & Social Psychology*, 8, 377–83.

Dohrenwend, B. P. and Dohrenwend, B. S. (1967), 'Field studies of social factors in relation to three types of psychological disorder', *Journal of Abnormal Psychology*, 72, 369–78.

De Paor, L. (1970), *Divided Ulster*, Harmondsworth : Pelican.

Deutsch, M. and Collins, M. E. (1951), *Interracial Housing: A Psychological Evaluation of a Social Experiment*, Minneapolis : University of Minnesota Press.

Devlin, P. (1975), *The Fall of the Northern Ireland Executive*, Belfast : Paddy Devlin, 39 Greenane, Shaw's Road.

Dillon, M. and Lehane, D. (1973), *Political Murder in Northern Ireland*, Harmondsworth : Penguin.

Davis, E. E. and Sinnott, R. (1979), *Attitudes in the Republic of Ireland Relevant to the Northern Ireland Problem: Volume 1*, Dublin: The Economic and Social Research Institute, Paper No. 97.

Dubos, R. (1965), *Man Adapting*, New Haven, Connecticut : Yale University Press.

Dudley Edwards, O. (1970), 'A look at the Reverend Ian Paisley', *Nusight*, May 1970, 11–16.

Duy San, N. (1969), 'Psychiatry in the army of the Republic of

Viet Nam', in P. G. Bourne (ed.), *The Psychology and Physiology of Stress*, New York : Academic Press.

Elliot, R. S. P. and Hickie, J. (1971), *Ulster. A Case Study of Conflict Theory*, London : Longman.

Elliott, P. (1976), *Reporting in Northern Ireland: a Study of News in Britain, Ulster and the Irish Republic*, University of Leicester : Centre for Mass Communication Research.

Elliott, R. and Lockhart, W. H. (in press), 'Characteristics of scheduled offenders and juvenile delinquents', in J. I. Harbison and J. J. M. Harbison (eds), *Children and Young People in Northern Ireland*, London : Open Books.

Elliott, S. (1973), *Northern Ireland Parliamentary Election Results 1921–1972*, Chichester : Political Reference Publications.

Elms, A. C. (1972), *Social Psychology and Social Relevance*, Boston : Little, Brown & Co.

Elms, A. C. (1976), *Personality in Politics*, New York : Harcourt Brace Jovanovich.

Evason, E. (1976), *Poverty: The Facts in Northern Ireland*, London : Child Poverty Action Group.

Eysenck, H. J. (1975), 'The Structure of Social Attitudes', *British Journal of Social and Clinical Psychology*, 14, 322–31.

Fahy, P. A. (1971), 'Some political behaviour patterns and attitudes of Roman Catholic priests in a rural part of Northern Ireland', *Economic & Social Review*, 3, No. 1.

Fee, F. (1976), *Reading and Disturbance in Belfast Schools*, Belfast Education and Library Board.

Festinger, L. (1957) *A Theory of Cognitive Dissonance.* New York : Harper & Row.

Festinger, L. (1964) *Conflict, Decision and Dissonance.* Stanford, Calif. : Stanford University Press.

Fiedler, F. E. (1965) The contingency model : a theory of leadership effectiveness, in H. Proshansky & B. Seidenberg (eds) *Basic Studies in Social Psychology.* New York : Holt, Rinehart & Winston.

Foley, M. (1973), *Report to the People of Ballymurphy.*

Fortnight (1973a), 'Daz & Omo : the propaganda war', *Fortnight*, 61, 8–9, 4 May.

Fortnight (1973b), 'Is integrated education on the way?', *Fortnight*, 55, 6–9, 1 February.

Fortnight (1973c), 'Education, Practical . . .', *Fortnight*, 57, 8–9, 2 March.

Foulds, G. A. (1965), *Personality and Personal Illness*, London : Tavistock Publications.

Fraser, R. M. (1971a), 'Ulster's children of conflict', *New Society*, April 15, 17 (446), 630–3.

Fraser, R. M. (1971b), 'The cost of commotion—analysis of psychiatric sequelae of 1969 Belfast riots', *British Journal of Psychiatry*, 118 (544), 257–64.

Fraser, R. M. (1972), 'At school during guerilla war', *Special Education*, 61 (2), 6–8.

Fraser, R. M. (1974), *Children in Conflict*, Harmondsworth: Pelican.

French, J. R. P. Jr. and Raven, B. H. (1959), 'The bases of social power', in D. Cartwright (ed.), *Studies in Social Power*, Ann Arbor, Mich.: University of Michigan Press.

Freud, S. (1917), 'Mourning and Melancholia', in *Collected Papers*, Vol. 4, London: Hogarth Press and the Institute of Psychoanalysis, 1950, 152–72.

Friedlander, R. A. (1978), 'Terrorism and Political Violence', in M. H. Livingston (ed.), *International Terrorism in the Contemporary World*, London: Greenwood Press.

Gibb, C. A. (ed.), (1969), *Leadership: Selected Readings*, Harmondsworth: Penguin.

Gibson, N. (1971), 'The Northern problem. Religious or economic or what?' *Community Forum*, 1.(1) 2–5.

Gibson, N. (1974), *Economic and social implications of the political alternatives that may be open to Northern Ireland*, New University of Ulster.

Glass, D. C. and Singer, J. E. (1972), *Urban Stress: Experiments on Noise and Social Stressors*, New York: Academic Press.

Gray, T. (1966), *The Irish Answer: An Anatomy of Modern Ireland*, London: Heinemann.

Gray, T. (1972), *The Orange Order*, London: Bodley.

Hammond, W. A. (1883), *A Treatise on Insanity in its Medical Relations*, United Kingdom: Lewis.

Harbinson, J. F. (1973), *The Ulster Unionist Party, 1882–1973*, Belfast: Blackstaff Press.

Harding, J., Proshansky, H., Kutner, B. and Chein, I. (1969), 'Prejudice and ethnic relations', in G. Lindzey and E. Aronson (eds) *Handbook of Social Psychology* (2nd ed.), V.5, 1–76, Reading, Mass.: Addison-Wesley.

Hare, R. D. (1970), *Psychopathy: Theory and Research*, London: Wiley.

Harris, A. (1941), 'Psychiatric reactions of civilians in war-time', *Lancet*, 2, 152–5.

Harris, R. (1972), *Prejudice and Tolerance in Ulster*, Manchester: Manchester University Press.

Heider, F. (1946), 'Attitudes and cognitive organisation', *Journal of Psychology*, 21, 107–12.

Hemphill, R. E. (1941), 'The influence of war on mental disease', *Journal of Mental Science*, 87, 170–82.

Hinkle, L. E. and Wolff, H. G. (1958), 'Ecologic investigation of the relationship between illness, life experience and the social environment', *Annals of Internal Medicine*, 49 (6), 1373–88.

Hofstander, R. (1965), *The Paranoid Style in American Politics*, New York : Knopf.

Hoggart, S. (1973), 'The army PR men of Northern Ireland', *New Society*, 11 October, 26 (575), 79–80.

Hollander, E. P. (1958), 'Conformity, status and idiosyncrasy credit', *Psychological Review*, 65, 117–27.

Hollander, E. P. (1964), *Leaders, Groups and Influence*, New York : Oxford University Press.

Hollander, E. P. (1976), *Principles and Methods of Social Psychology*, New York : Oxford University Press.

Hollander, E. P. and Julian, J. W. (1969), 'Contemporary trends in the analysis of leadership processes'. *Psychological Bulletin*, 71, 387–97.

Hollander, E. P. and Julian, J. W. (1970), 'Studies in leader legitimacy, influence and innovations', in L. Berkowitz, (ed.), *Advances in Experimental Social Psychology*, New York : Academic Press.

Homans, G. C. (1961), *Social Behaviour: its Elementary Forms*, New York : Harcourt Brace.

Hopkins, F. (1943), 'Decrease in admission to mental observation wards during the war', *British Medical Journal*, 1, 358.

Horowitz, E. L. (1936), 'The development of attitude toward the Negro', Archives of Psychology in New York, 194, cited in J. Harding, H. Proshansky, B. Kutner and I. Chein, 'Prejudice and ethnic relations', in G. Lindzey and E. Aronson (eds), *Handbook of Social Psychology* (2nd ed.), V5, 1–76, Reading, Mass. : Addison-Wesley.

Howe, M. J. (1977), *Television and Children*, London : New University Education.

Hyman, H. H. and Sheatsley, P. B. (1964), 'Attitudes toward desegregation', *Scientific American*, 211, 16–23.

Inside Story (1972), *Northern Ireland* (Special Issue), London : Inside Story.

Jahoda, G. and Harrison, S. (1975), 'Belfast Children : some effects of a conflict environment', *Irish Journal of Psychology*, 3, 1–19.

Jardine, E., Curran, J. D. and Harbison, J. (1978), 'Young offenders and their offences : some comparisons between Northern Ireland,

England and Scotland', paper presented to the Northern Ireland Regional Office, British Psychological Society Conference on Children and Young People in a Society under Stress, Belfast, September 1978.

Jenvey, S. (1972), 'Sons and haters—Ulster youth in conflict', *New Society*, 20 July, 21 (512), 125–7.

Katz, D. (1960), 'The functional approach to the study of attitudes', *Public Opinion Quarterly*, 24, 163–204.

Katz, P. A. (1973), 'Perception of racial cues in pre-school children : a new look', *Developmental Psychology*, 8, 295–9.

Katz, P. A. (1976), *Towards the Elimination of Racism*, New York : Pergamon Press.

Katz, P. A. and Seavey, C. (1973), 'Labels and children's perception of faces', *Child Development*, 44, 770–5.

Katz, P. A. and Zalk, S. R. (1974), 'Doll preferences : an index of racial attitudes?' *Journal of Educational Psychology*, 66, 663–8.

Kilham, W. and Mann, L. (1974), 'Level of destructive obedience as a function of the transmitter and executant roles in the Milgram obedience paradigm', *Journal of Personality and Social Psychology*, 29, 696–702.

Laqueur, W. (1977), *Terrorism*, London : Weidenfeld and Nicolson.

Latané, B. and Darley, J. M. (1968), 'Group inhibition of bystander intervention in emergencies', *Journal of Personality & Social Psychology*, 10, 215–21.

Lazarus, R. S. (1966), *Psychological Stress and the Coping Process*, New York : McGraw-Hill.

Lebow, R. N. (1976), *White Britain and Black Ireland: the Influence of Stereotypes on Colonial Policy*, Philadelphia; Pa. : Institute for the Study of Human Issues.

Legrande du Saulle, H. (1871), 'De l'état mental des habitants de Paris pendant les événements de 1870–71', *Annales Medico-Psychologiques*, 11, 222–41.

Lerner, M. J. (1965), 'The effect of responsibility and choice on a partner's attractiveness following failure', *Journal of Personality*, 33, 178–87.

Lerner, M. J. and Simmons, C. H. (1966), 'Observer's reaction to the "innocent victim" : compassion or rejection?' *Journal of Personality and Social Psychology*, 4, 203–10.

Lerner, R. M., Solomon, H. and Brody, S. (1971), 'Helping behaviour at a bus stop', *Psychological Reports*, 28, 200.

Lewis, A. (1942), 'Incidence of neurosis in England under war conditions', *Lancet*, 2, 175–83.

Lifton, R. J. (1968), *Revolutionary Immortality*, New York : Vintage Books.

Lloyd, E. V. (1976), 'School children's ethnic attitudes towards the denominational names in Northern Ireland', unpublished B.Sc. thesis, New University of Ulster.

Lundquist, G. (1945), 'Prognosis and course in manic-depressive psychoses', *Acta Psychiatrica Neurological Supplement No. 35.*

Lyons, H. A. (1971a), 'Psychiatric sequelae of the Belfast riots', *British Journal of Psychiatry*, 118 (544), 265–73.

Lyons, H. A. (1971b), 'The psychiatric effects of civil disturbances', *World Medicine*, 21 April, 17–20.

Lyons, H. A. (1972a), 'Depressive illness and aggression in Belfast', *British Medical Journal*, 1 (5796), 342–4.

Lyons, H. A. (1972b), 'Psychiatric sequelae of the Belfast riots—Reply', *British Journal of Psychiatry*, 120 (557), 471.

Lyons, H. A. (1972c), 'Riots and rioters in Belfast—demographic analysis of 1674 arrestees in a two-year period', *Economic & Social Review*, 3 (4), 605–14.

Lyons, H. A. (1973a), 'Violence in Belfast—a review of the psychological effects', *Public Health*, 87, 231–8.

Lyons, H. A. (1973b), 'Violence in Belfast—a review of the psychological effects', *Community Health*, 5 (3), 163–8.

Lyons, H. A. (1973c), 'The psychological effects of civil disturbances on children', *Northern Teacher*, Belfast, Winter, 35–8.

Lyons, H. A. (1974a), 'The psychological effects of the civil disturbances', *Aquarius*, 11–14.

Lyons, H. A. (1974b), 'Terrorist bombing and the psychological sequelae', *Journal of the Irish Medical Association*, 67 (1), 15–19

Lyons, H. A. (1975), 'Legacy of violence in Northern Ireland', *International Journal of Offender Therapy & Comparative Criminology*, 19 (3), 292–8.

McAllister, I. (1977), *The Northern Ireland Social Democratic and Labour Party: Political Opposition in a Divided Society*, London : Macmillan.

McCann, E. (1971), *The British Press and Northern Ireland*, London : Northern Ireland Socialist Research Centre.

McClosky, H. (1958), 'Conservatism and personality', *American Political Science Review*, 52, 27–45.

McCord, W. and McCord, J. (1964), *The Psychopath: An Essay on the Criminal Mind*, Princeton, N.J. : Van Nostrand.

MacGreil, M. (1977), *Prejudice and Tolerance in Ireland*, Dublin : College of Industrial Relations.

McGuire, M. (1973), *To Take Arms: A Year in the Provisional IRA*, London : Macmillan.

MacKenzie, B. K. (1948), 'The importance of contact in determining attitudes towards Negroes', *Journal of Abnormal and Social Psychology*, 43, 417–41.

McKernan, J. (in press), 'Pupil values as social indicators of intergroup differences in Northern Ireland', in J. I. Harbison and J. J. M. Harbison (eds), *Children and Young People in Northern Ireland*, London : Open Books.

McPhail, P., Ungoed–Thomas, J. R. and Chapman, H. (1972), *Moral Education in the Secondary School*, London : Longman.

MacStiofain, S. (1975), *Revolutionary in Ireland*, London : Gordon Cremonesi.

Mallin, J. (1978), 'Terrorism as a Military Weapon', in M. H. Livingston (ed.), *International Terrorism in the Contemporary World*, London : Greenwood Press.

Mann, J. H. (1959), 'The effects of interracial contact on sociometric choices and perceptions', *Journal of Social Psychology*, 50, 143–52.

Mann, R. D. (1959), 'A review of the relationships between personality and performance in small groups', *Psychological Bulletin*, 56, 241–70.

Marcus, P. M. (1960), 'Expressive and instrumental groups : toward a theory of group structure', *American Journal of Sociology*, 66, 54–9.

Markham, S. (1971), *What About the Irish?*, London : Runnymede Trust.

Marrinan, P. (1973), *Paisley: Man of Wrath*, Tralee : Anvil Books.

Massey, A. (1941), 'Report of meeting at Tavistock Clinic', *British Medical Journal*, 1, 77.

Mickolus, E. (1978), 'Trends in Transnational Terrorism', in M. H. Livingston (ed.), *International Terrorism in the Contemporary World*, London : Greenwood Press.

Middleton, M. R., Tajfel, H. and Johnson, M. B.(1970), 'Cognitive and affective aspects of children's national attitudes', *British Journal of Social and Clinical Psychology*, 9, 122–34.

Milgram, S. (1970), 'The experience of living in cities', *Science*, 13, 1461–8.

Milgram, S. (1974), *Obedience to Authority*, London : Tavistock.

Miller, R. (1978), *Attitudes to Work in Northern Ireland*, Belfast : Fair Employment Agency.

Miller, W. A. (1978), 'Who are the British?' *Fortnight*, October, 171, 16–17.

Minard, R. D. (1952), 'Race relations in the Pocahontas coal field', *Journal of Social Issues*, 8, 29–44.

Mira, E. (1939), 'Psychiatric experiences in the Spanish Civil War', *British Medical Journal*, 1, 1217–20.

Mons, W. E. M. (1941), 'Air-raids and the child', *Lancet*, 2, 625–6.

Moxon-Browne, E. P. (1979), Northern Ireland Attitude Survey—Main Survey. Belfast : Queen's University (Unpublished, mimeographed report).

Nadel, G. (1977), 'Just about all talk and no action', *TV Guide*, 8 October.

Nelson, S. (1975), 'Protestant "ideology" considered : the case of "discrimination" ', in I. Crewe (ed.), *British Sociology Yearbook Volume 2. The Politics of Race*, 155–87, London : Croom Helm.

Newcomb, T. M. (1943), *Personality and Social Change: Attitude Formation in a Student Community*, New York : Dryden.

Newcomb, T. M. (1953), 'An approach to the study of communicative acts', *Psychological Review*, 60, 393–404.

Nusight (1969), 'A profile of Reverend Ian Paisley', *Nusight*, October, 10–12.

Nusight, (1969), 'The phenomenon of Paisleyism', *Nusight*, October, 13–15.

O'Connor, K. (1974), *The Irish in Britain*, Dublin : Torc.

O'Donnell, E. E. (1977), *Northern Irish Stereotypes*, Dublin : College of Industrial Relations.

O'Farrell, P. (1975), *England and Ireland since 1800*, New York : Oxford University Press.

O'Malley, P. P. (1972), 'Attempted suicide before and after the communal violence in Belfast, August 1969 : a preliminary study', *Journal of the Irish Medical Association*, 65 (5), 109–13.

O'Malley, P. P. (1975), 'Attempted suicide, suicide and communal violence', *Irish Medical Journal*, 68 (5), 103–109.

O'Neill, T. M. (1972), *The Autobiography of Terence O'Neill*, London : Rupert Hart-Davis.

Osgood, C. E. (1962), *An Alternative to War or Surrender*, Urbana : University of Illinois Press.

Osgood, C. E. (1965), 'Escalation as a strategy', *War/Peace Reports*, 5, 12–14.

Osgood, C. E. and Tannenbaum, P. H. (1955), 'The principle of congruity in the prediction of attitude change', *Psychological Review*, 62, 42–55.

Overy, R. (1972), 'Children's play', *Community Forum*, 2.

Paxman, J. (1978), 'Reporting failure in Ulster', *The Listener*, 5 October, 429–30.

Pegg, G. (1940), 'Psychiatric casualties in London, September 1940', *British Medical Journal*, 2, 553–5.

Pettigrew, T. F. (1961), 'Social psychology and desegregation research', *American Psychologist*, 16, 105–12.

Pettigrew, T. F. (1971), *Racially Separate or Together?* New York : McGraw–Hill.

Pokorny, A. D. (1964), 'Suicide rates in various psychiatric disorders', *Journal of Nervous & Mental Diseases*, 139, 499–506.

Rennie, T. (1942), 'Prognosis in manic-depressive psychoses', *American Journal of Psychiatry*, 98, 801–14.

Report of the Interdepartmental Committee on Matters Relating to the Alienation of Young People (1974), Belfast : Northern Ireland Civil Service.

Research Report (1976), *Suitability of Boys for Training School*, Belfast : Statistics and Economics Unit, Department of Finance.

Robinson, A. (1971), 'Education and sectarian conflict in Northern Ireland', *New Era*, January.

Roche, D. J. D., Birrell, W. D. and Greer, J. E. (1975), 'A sociopolitical profile of clergymen in Northern Ireland', *Social Studies*, 4 (2), 143–51.

Rokeach, M. (1954), 'The nature and meaning of dogmatism', *Psychological Review*, 61, 194–205.

Rokeach, M. (1960), *The Open and Closed Mind*, New York : Basic Books.

Rokeach, M. (1973), *The Nature of Human Values*, New York : Free Press.

Rose, R. (1971), *Governing without Consensus. An Irish Perspective*, London : Faber & Faber.

Rose, R. (1976), *Northern Ireland: A Time of Choice*, London : Macmillan.

Rose, R., McAllister, I. and Mair, P. (1978), *Is there a Concurring Majority about Northern Ireland?*, Glasgow : Centre for the Study of Public Policy, University of Strathclyde.

Rosen, E. and Gregory, I. (1965), *Abnormal Psychology*, Philadelphia : Saunders.

Russell, J. (1975), 'Violence and the Ulster Schoolboy', *New Society*, 26 July, 25 (564), 204–206.

Rutherford, B. (1966), 'Psychopathology, decision making and political involvement', *Journal of Conflict Resolution*, 10, 387–407.

Rutter, M., Tizard, J. and Whitmore, K. (1970), *Education, Health and Behaviour*, London : Longman.

Ryan, W. (1976), *Blaming the Victim*, New York : Vintage Books.

Sanford, F. H. (1950), *Authoritarianism and Leadership*, Philadelphia : Institute for Research in Human Relations.

Schellenberg, J. A. (1977), 'Area variations of violence in Northern Ireland', *Sociological Focus*, 10 (1), 73.

Schmidt, H. D. (1960), 'Bigotry in Schoolchildren', *Commentary*, 29, 253-7.

Schlesinger, P. (1978), *Putting 'Reality' Together*, London : Constable.

Schwartz, S. H. and Clausen, G. T. (1970), 'Responsibility, norms and helping in an emergency', *Journal of Personality and Social Psychology*, 16, 299-310.

Scott, F. E. (1976), 'The political preaching tradition in Ulster : prelude to Paisley', *Western Speech Communication*, 249-59.

Selye, H. (1956), *The Stress of Life*, New York : McGraw-Hill.

Severy, L. J., Brigham, J. C. and Schlenker, B. R. (1976), *A Contemporary Introduction to Social Psychology*, New York : McGraw-Hill.

Smith, M. B., Bruner, J. S. and White, R. W. (1956), *Opinions and Personality*, New York : Wiley.

Spencer, A. E. C. W. (1974), 'Urbanization and the problem of Ireland', *Aquarius*, 82-90.

Stogdill, R. M. (1948), 'Personal factors associated with leadership', *Journal of Psychology*, 25, 35-71.

Storr, A. (1968), *Human Aggression*, Harmondsworth : Penguin.

Storr, A. (1978), 'Sadism and Paranoia', in M. H. Livingston (ed.), *International Terrorism in the Contemporary World*, London : Greenwood Press.

Stouffer, S. A., Lumsdaine, A. A., Lumsdaine, M. H., Williams, R. M., Jr., Smith, M. B., Janis, I. L., Star, S. A. and Cottrell, L. S., Jr (1949), 'The American Soldier : Combat and its Aftermath', Vol 2 of *Studies in Social Psychology in World War II*, Princeton : Princeton University.

Sturge, C. (1972), 'Reading Retardation and Anti-Social Behaviour', unpublished M. Phil. thesis, University of London.

Sunday Times, Insight Team (1972), *Ulster*, Harmondsworth : Penguin.

Sweetman, R. (1972), *On Our Knees—Ireland 1972*, London : Pan Books.

Tajfel, H. (1969), 'Cognitive aspects of prejudice', *Journal of Social Issues*, 25, 79-97.

Tajfel, H., Nemeth, C., Jahoda, G., Campbell, J. D. and Johnson, M. B. (1970), 'The development of children's preference for their own country : a cross-national study', *International Journal of Psychology*, 5, 245–53.

Tajfel, H. and Jahoda, G. (1966), 'Development in children of concepts and attitudes about their own and other nations : a cross-national study', *Proceedings of the Eighteenth International Congress of Psychology*, Moscow, Symposium 36, 17–33.

Target, G. W. (1975), *Bernadette: the Story of Bernadette Devlin*, London : Hodder & Stoughton.

Taylor, L. and Nelson, S. (1977), *Young people and civil conflict in Northern Ireland*, Belfast : Department of Health and Social Services.

Temoche, A., Pugh, T. F. and McMahon, B. (1964), 'Suicides rates among current and former mental institution patients', *Journal of Nervous and Mental Diseases*, 136, 124–30.

Thompson, J. F. (1969), Personal communication to R. M. Fraser, 17 September. Quoted in Fraser (1971b).

Thompson, R. F. and Spencer, W. A. (1966), 'Habituation : a model phenomenon for the study of neuronal substrates of behaviour', *Psychological Review*, 73, 16–43.

Tischler, G. L. (1969), 'Patterns of psychiatric attrition and of behaviour in a combat zone', in P. G. Bourne (ed.), *The Psychology and Physiology of Stress*, New York : Academic Press.

Turk, H. (1961), 'Instrumental and expressive ratings reconsidered', *Sociometry*, 24, 76–81.

Ungoed-Thomas, J. R. (1972), 'Patterns of adolescent behaviour and relationships in Northern Ireland', *Journal of Moral Education*, 2 (1), 53–61.

Van Voris, W. H. (1975), *Violence in Ulster: an Oral Documentary*, Amherst : University of Massachusetts Press.

Vinacke, W. E. (1957), 'Stereotypes as social concepts', *Journal of Social Psychology*, 46, 229–43.

Wadesworth, M. E. J. (1975), 'Delinquency in a national sample of children', *British Journal of Criminology*, 15, 167–74.

Weber, M. (1921), 'The sociology of charismatic authority', in H. H. Gerth and C. W. Mills (trans and eds), (1946), From Max Weber, *Essays in Sociology*, New York : Oxford University Press.

West, D. and Farrington, D. (1973), *Who Becomes Delinquent?*, London : Heinemann.

Whale, J. (1973), 'Modern guerilla movements,' *Community Forum*, 3 (2), 3–6.

Whyte, J. (1978), 'Interpretations of the Northern Ireland problem : an appraisal', *Economic and Social Review*, 9, 257–82.

Whyte, J. H. (1971), *Church and State in Modern Ireland, 1923–1970*, Dublin : Gill and Macmillan.

Williams, R. M., Jr. (1964), *Strangers Next Door: Ethnics Relations in American Communities*, Englewood Cliffs, N. J. : Prentice-Hall.

Wilner, D. M., Walkley, R. P. and Cook, S. W. (1955), *Human Relations in Interracial Housing*, Minneapolis : University of Minnesota Press.

Wilson, G. D. (ed.) (1973), *The Psychology of Conservatism*, New York : Academic Press.

Winchester, S. (1974), *In Holy Terror*, London : Faber & Faber.

Wohlwill, J. F. (1966), 'The physical environment : a problem for a psychology of stimulation', *Journal of Social Issues*, 22, 29–38.

Wohlwill, J. F. (1970), 'The emerging discipline of environmental psychology', *American Psychologist*, 25, 303–12.

The World Almanac and Book of Facts (1978), New York : Newspaper Enterprise Association, Inc.

Wright, F. (1973), 'Protestant ideology and politics in Ulster', *European Journal of Sociology*, 14, 213–80.

Zimbardo, P. G., Haney, C., Banks, W. C. and Jaffe, D. (1973), 'The Psychology of Imprisonment : Privation, Power and Pathology', unpublished manuscript, Stanford, Calif. : Stanford University.

Index